A WORLD
SET APART

BOOKS BY MARCIA MUTH

Is It Safe To Drink The Water? A Guide To Santa Fe

How To Paint & Sell Your Art

Kachinas: A Selected Bibliography

Writing And Selling Poetry, Fiction, Articles, Plays and Local History

Thin Ice And Other Poems

Indian Pottery Of The Southwest: A Selected Bibliography

Sticks And Stones And Other Poems

Words And Images

A WORLD SET APART

Memory Paintings

by

MARCIA MUTH

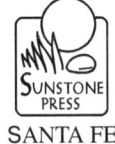

SUNSTONE PRESS

SANTA FE

Book and cover design by Vicki Ahl

Sunstone books may be purchased for educational, business, or sales promotional use. For information please write: Special Markets Department, Sunstone Press, P.O. Box 2321, Santa Fe, New Mexico 87504-2321.

Library of Congress Cataloging-in-Publication Data:

Muth, Marcia, 1919-
  A world set apart : memory paintings / by Marcia Muth.
      p. cm.
  ISBN 0-86534-526-0 (softcover : alk. paper)
  1. Muth, Marcia, 1919- 2. Painters--United States--Biography.
  3. Art and society--United States--History--20th century. I. Title.

ND237.M94A2 2007
759.13--dc22

                                        2006034231

WWW.SUNSTONEPRESS.COM
SUNSTONE PRESS / POST OFFICE BOX 2321 / SANTA FE, NM 87504-2321 /USA
(505) 988-4418 / ORDERS ONLY (800) 243-5644 / FAX (505) 988-1025

For all my collectors everywhere. Your interest in my work and encouragement are sources of inspiration to me. Thank you very much.

PREFACE

When I started planning this book, I looked up the words "memory painting" in a dictionary of art terms and was directed to "mind's eye," the faculty of the mind to imagine or remember visual things. That is precisely what these paintings are all about but I must add this caveat: none of them are about an actual place. They are all based on the reality of life as I knew it in the 1930s, but they came from my imagination.

I am often asked "Why the thirties?" Why? Partly because I think that it was a very special time in the United States and partly because it was my time of growing up. It was a time of new inventions, new technology and freedom to explore and open up new territories in art, literature and music. There was also a feeling of neighborliness and mutual respect. I have tried to capture on canvas some of the places and activities of those times. The thirties were also a time of transition, combining the past with the latest and newest. Many homes still had and used their Victrolas while also enjoying radios. There were automobiles and trucks but some businesses still used horses and wagons.

I selected the painting "Merry-Go-Round" as an introduction to the book as a kind of symbol or metaphor for the thirties. Merry-Go-Rounds were a popular and inexpensive form of entertainment. No matter what their physical condition was they seemed colorful and exotic. Riding on the animals was living a dream. This is the only painting I have done on which I also wrote a poem and a date.

We spend our lives on the Merry-Go-Round Riding the
*   animals of our choice, our ears are filled with its music*
*   Spinning, Spinning faster and faster*
Until the landscape is blurred and memory falters
*   It stops*
At last, it stops and we, poor weary riders
*   Stumble off*
*   Trembling at strange new sights.*

Looking back, I can see how appropriate the poem is for the time of the thirties. Those years were part of a twenty year intermezzo between two great wars. Like the riders our ears were so filled with the music of the present that we did not hear the ominous drum sound of the future.

I am often asked questions that are specific to my painting. One is "how do you decide what to paint?" I am quick to say that there is no lack of ideas. Ideas for paintings can come from the memory of a place, a situation or special event. There are always suggestions from family, friends, even strangers.

I am also asked about the names and numbers in my paintings. I "borrow" the names of family and friends including birthdates, telephone numbers and street addresses. Sometimes I use the date of the day I am painting. And whenever I can, I use my birth year, 1919. In some cases I make up names for products and places. I have only used my name once for a store and that was by request from the person who had commissioned the work.

A few years ago I started using canvas with wide stretcher edges so I could continue the painting around the canvas edges. In my mind, the painting goes on beyond the physical barriers. I always include as much detail as is needed to convey what I want the viewers to see in the painting. The details are the language of the painting.

I was not a child prodigy. I started painting in 1974. As a self-taught artist, painting has always been and continues to be a learning experience. Painting is a way of life for me and yes, I still paint every day.

—Marcia Muth

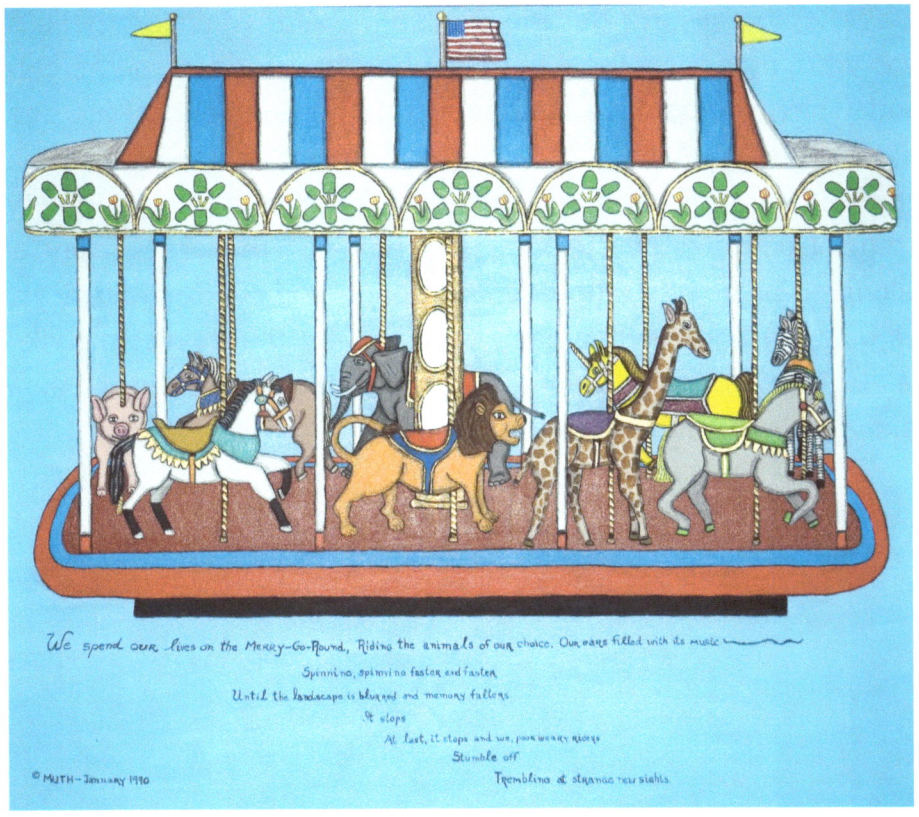

One of the first enterprises to spring up after automobiles were more common was the gas station. The *A-One Garage* represents a typical neighborhood gas station of the thirties. Not only gas was dispensed but it was the place for car repairs, especially for getting flat tires fixed. Most of these stations were owned by local people who often lived in the neighborhood. They also sold ice cold pop (5¢) kept in a kind of ice chest. You helped yourself to the limited choices, strawberry, orange and root beer. The stations offered free maps, free air and served as social centers for the men and boys of the area. They also welcomed bicyclists who needed repairs and air for their tires. In this painting another business is shown by the delivery truck for the "Golden Glow Dry Cleaners" for in those days the dry cleaners picked up and returned your clothes.

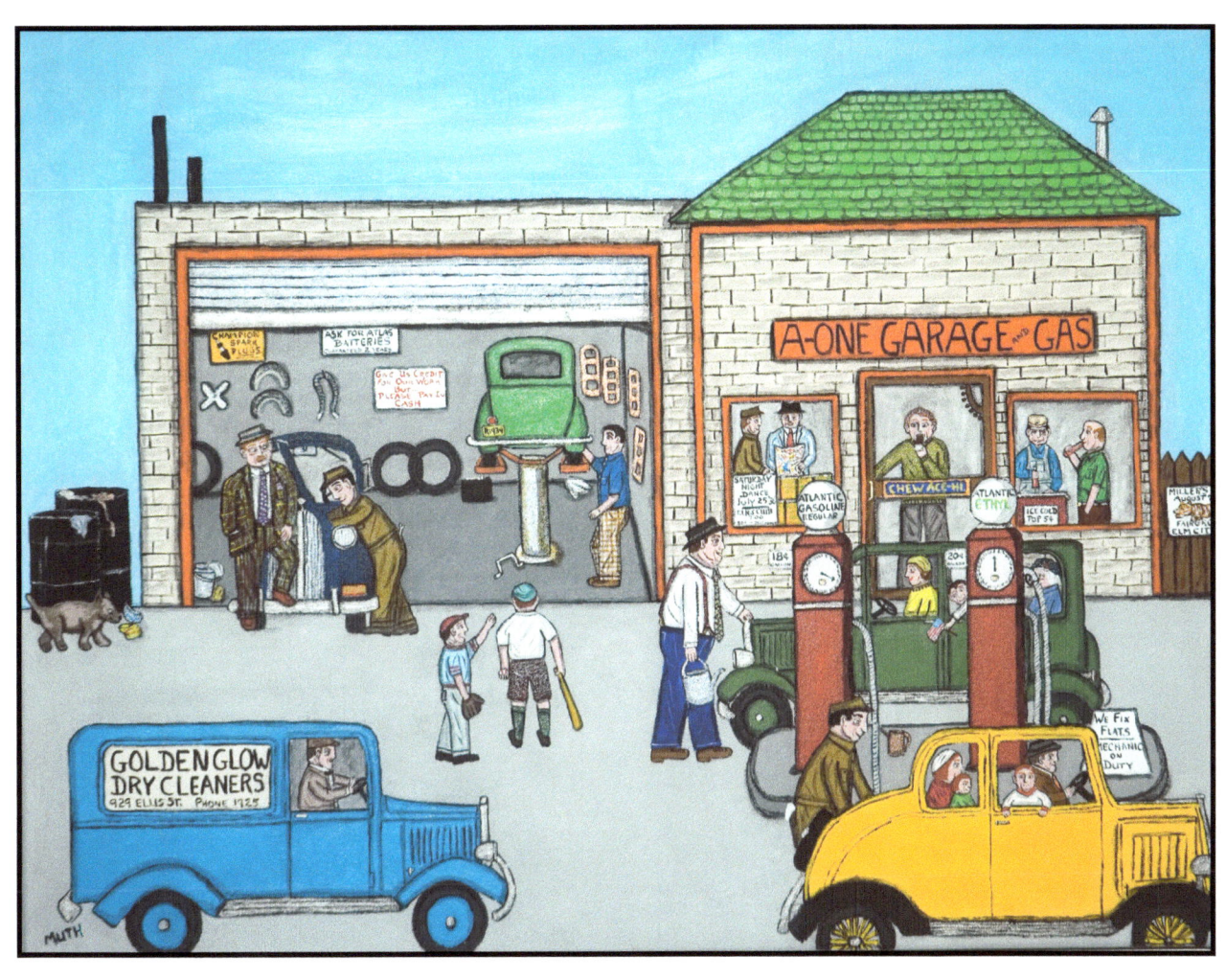

A-One Garage, 1992, acrylic on canvas, 18 x 24 inches
(Collection of Marilyn Fisher and Willard Chilcott)

This painting represents a landmark bookstore that was in Santa Fe, New Mexico for many years. The painting is based on my personal memories and that of one of the former owners, Roslyn Eisenberg. However, I decided to set it in the thirties so all the book titles reflect that. There are a few imaginary titles here and there. The windows did look out on the flower garden. Unlike today's large mega-stores, the Villagra was an example of the earlier stores, locally owned by a lover of books with a strong interest in the history, literature and folklore of the area. The owners read book reviews and would call customers to let them know when a book was coming out that would be of interest to them.

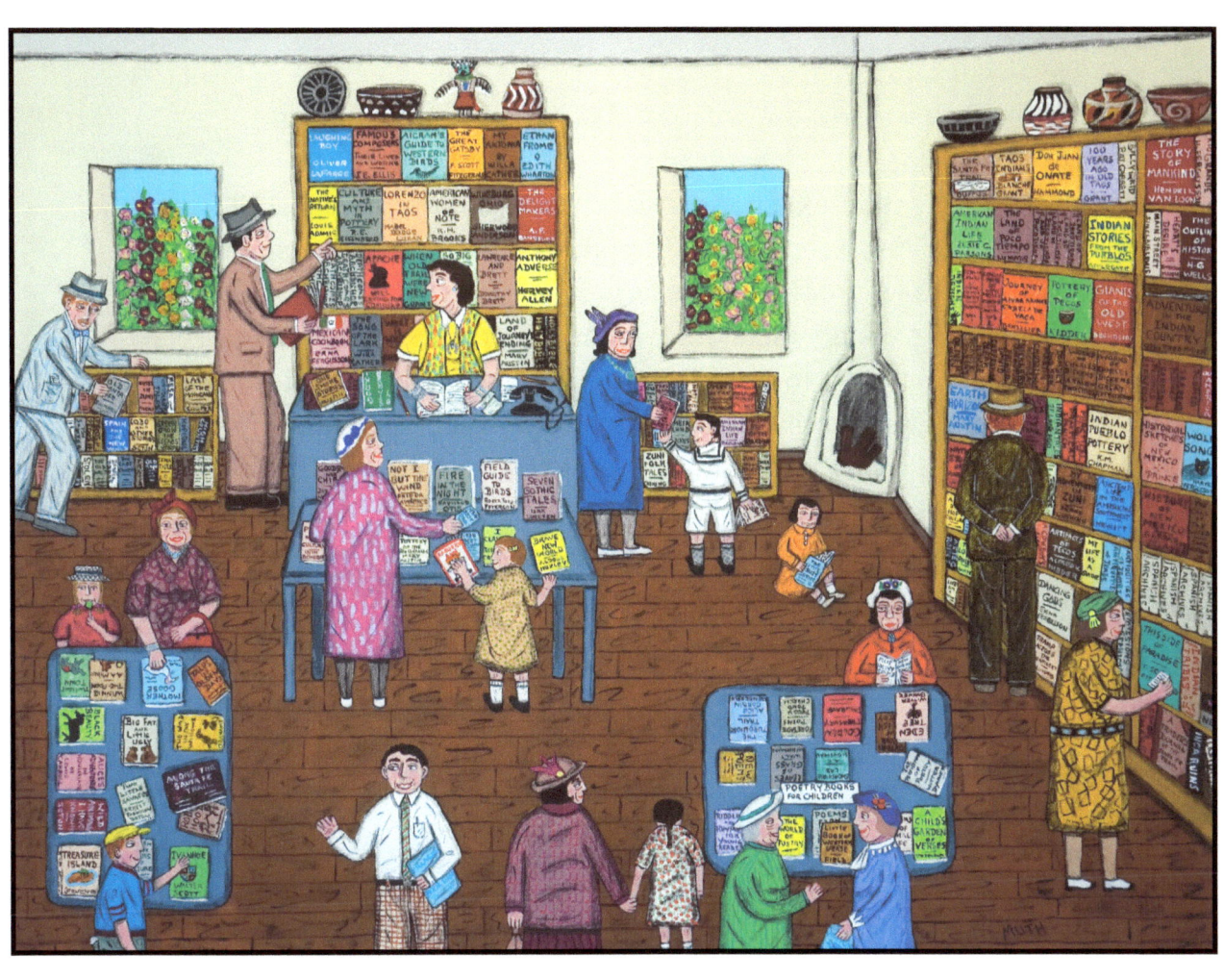

Villagra Book Store, 2000, acrylic on canvas, 18 x 24 inches
(Collection of Roslyn Eisenberg)

My actual experience with hotels did not begin until I was in my twenties. Before that they were only something I saw from the passing street car, read about, saw in movies or gleaned facts from post cards sent by traveling relatives. It was easy to imagine them as both places of delight and mystery. This painting shows a typically diverse group of people temporarily brought together in a new and strange environment. There are salesmen, families on vacation, convention attendees and hotel workers. I tried to convey that mixture of feeling in a hotel lobby—there is activity and anticipation and also there is quietness and waiting.

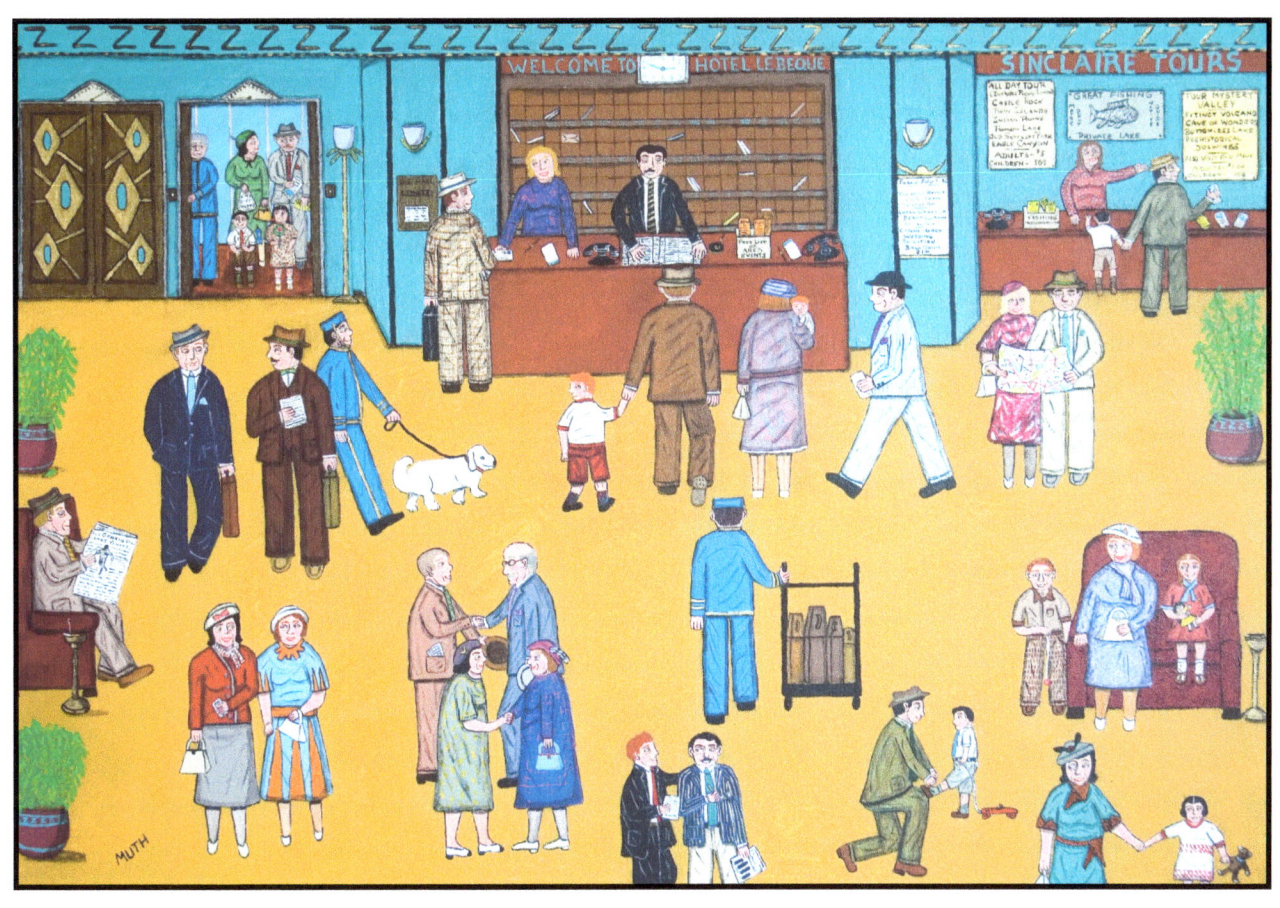

Lobby - Hotel LeBeque, 2003, acrylic on canvas, 24 x 36 inches
(Collection of the Artist)

During the thirties our main source of amusement came from the movies. However, the movies not only entertained us, they also were our connection with the world at large. Every movie house showed newsreels that kept us up to date on news at home and abroad. There were small movie houses in most neighborhoods and larger cities had big and elaborate movie houses which frequently represented Hollywood's ideas of a palace. These were first run houses which also included with the usual movie fare, a vaudeville show. Most of these had a large organ that rose up and burst into full musical glory to a wide and appreciative audience. Going to such a place was an adventure and special occasion. You bought your ticket from a windowed area, gave your ticket to a ticket taker as you entered the building and were shown to your seat by an usher or usherette. They were all in quasi-military uniforms and sported flashlights to aid latecomers. In those days you did not go to the movies to eat, you were there to see the stars. Neighborhood and small town theaters were more informal but they too sported names like Paramount, Rialto and Majestic. First-run houses charged 60 cents but smaller houses charged from 15¢ to 35¢. Matinees were popular and always featured lower prices. Why were the movies such an important part of our lives in the thirties? They were to many people an escape from the hard facts of reality. My painting shows a typical city scene with the movie theater as a focal point. Judging from the information on the marquee it was not a first-run house for the matinee price is 20¢ and it also is advertising "Bank Night." The smaller movie houses depended on various gimmicks to ensure steady audiences. Bank night involved a chance to win money. The lucky winner was chosen at random from ticket stubs. The winner had to be present to win. In the painting the theater is surrounded by a luncheonette, a barber shop, a beauty college salon and a dance studio. These would all be home-owned—what we used to call "mom and pop" shops. If they were limited in their resources, they were modest in their

16

prices. By the way, Saturday afternoon was the time of veritable parades of children to the neighborhood movies where for 10¢ you had an afternoon of fun and adventure. There was a comedy or cartoon, a serial episode, and a thrilling Western. Sometimes they also showed the newsreel or a short travel movie.

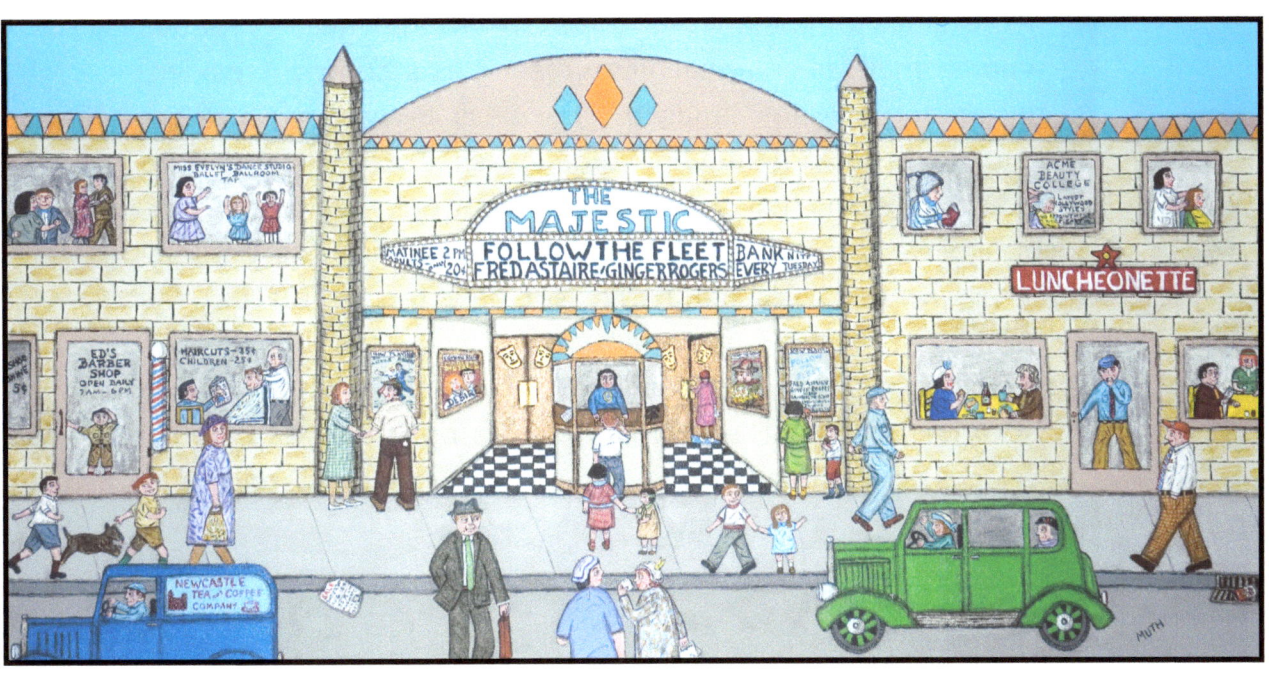

Majestic Theater Block, 2003, acrylic on canvas, 18 x 36 inches
(Collection of Kay Lockridge and Roslyn K. Pulitzer)

In the cities of the thirties there were older neighborhoods where small commercial ventures co-existed with residential property. Many times the business owners lived above their stores or restaurants. In some cases apartments or light housekeeping rooms had been made. While trucks were common, horses and wagons were still used. In the painting the horse & wagon are from the ice company. Not only the streets but the sidewalks were busy. People walked from place to place or took the street car. Children played on the sidewalk, people stopped to visit or argue politics. There were taxicabs but this was only for special occasions. A common sight, as seen in the painting, was a policeman walking his beat.

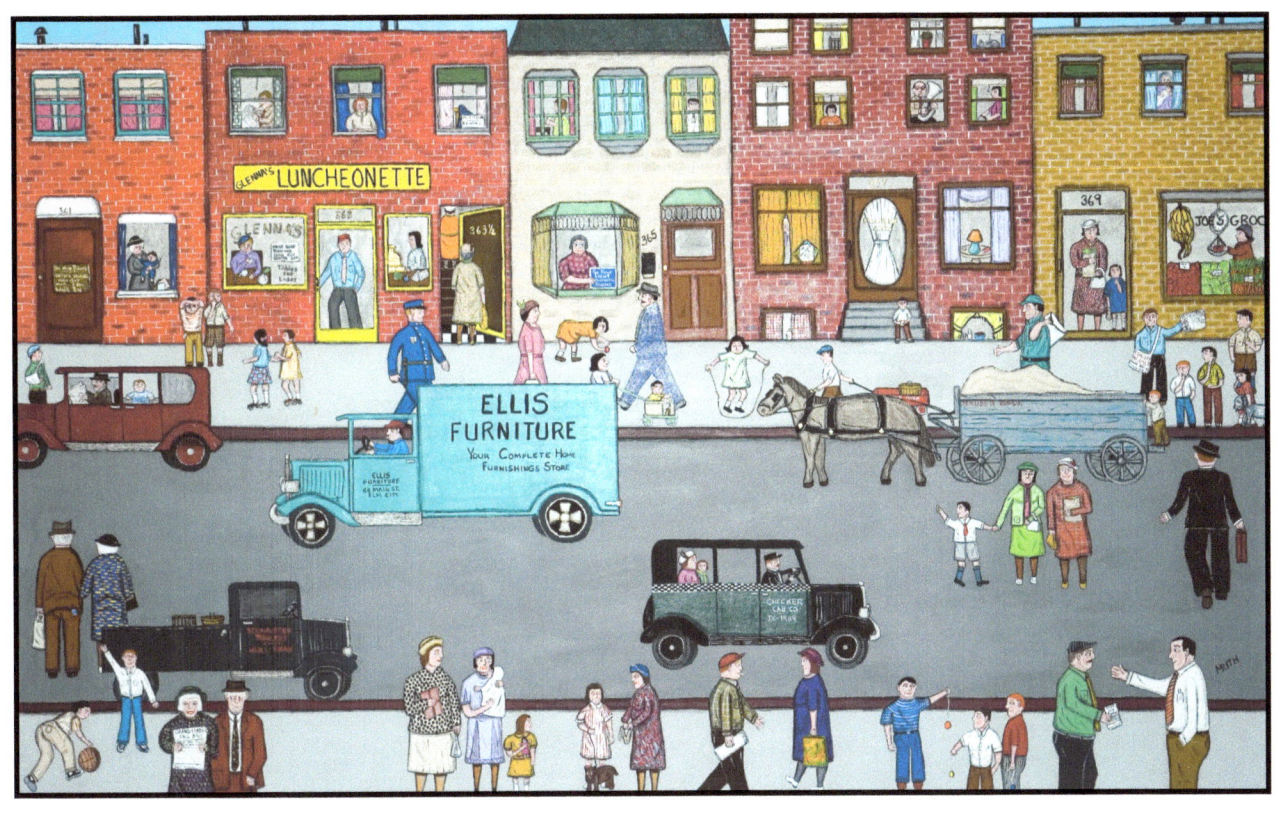

Franklin Street, 1989, acrylic on canvas, 30 x 60 inches
(Collection of Marilyn Fisher and Willard Chilcott)

Music played a large part in the lives of people in the thirties. Some of it came from radio programs but most of it was made by people. Nearly every home had a piano and someone in the family who played. There were records and record players. In the large cities, there were symphony orchestras and opera houses. In the smaller cities, orchestras were frequently "community" orchestras. In the major orchestras, there were no women musicians, except for an occasional harpist. In my paintings of orchestras I have included women. Actually, this could represent a symphony orchestra concert at any time. The soloist is playing a piano concerto.

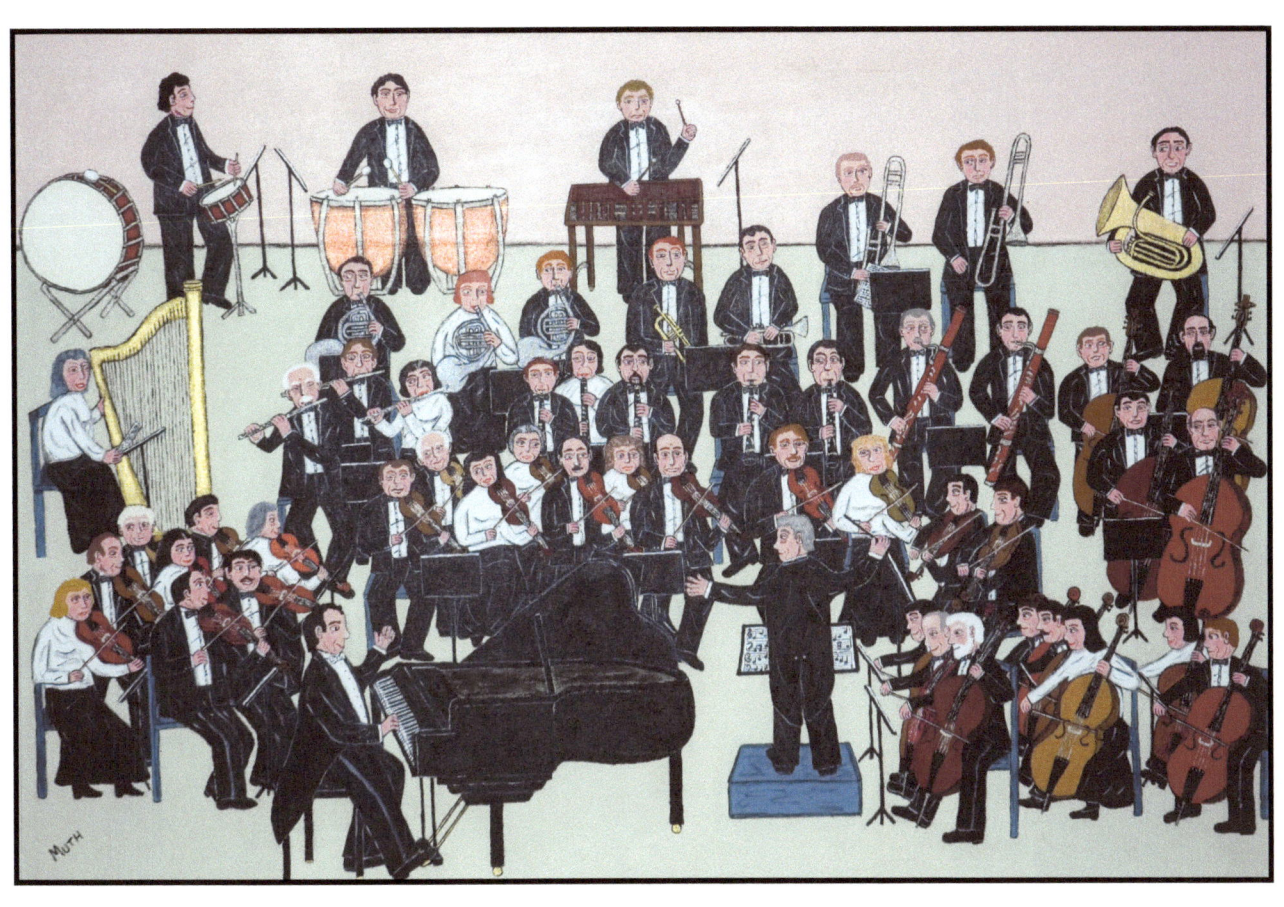

Orchestra, 2000, acrylic on canvas, 24 x 36 inches
(Collection of Marilyn Fisher and Willard Chilcott)

In this painting I have again included women players. In this one, the soloist is playing a cello concerto.

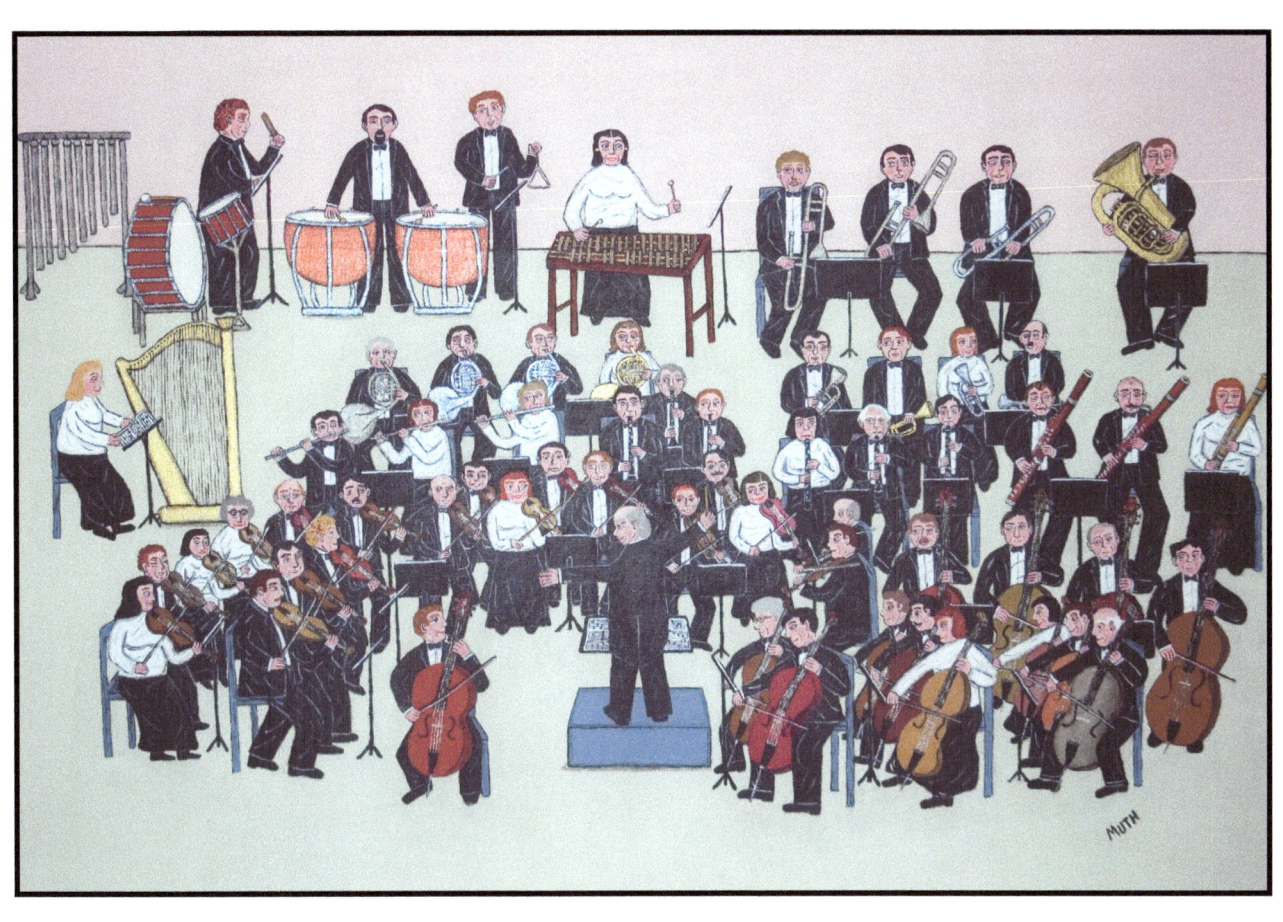

Cello Concerto, 2002, acrylic on canvas, 24 x 36 inches *(Private Collection)*

This shows the orchestra before the rehearsal actually starts. Again it is a scene in the thirties—all the women are in dresses. There is a certain informality about the scene. Some players are practicing, some are just arriving and a few are visiting. From the lack of tension in the air and the apparent affability of the conductor, this represents a community or regional orchestra.

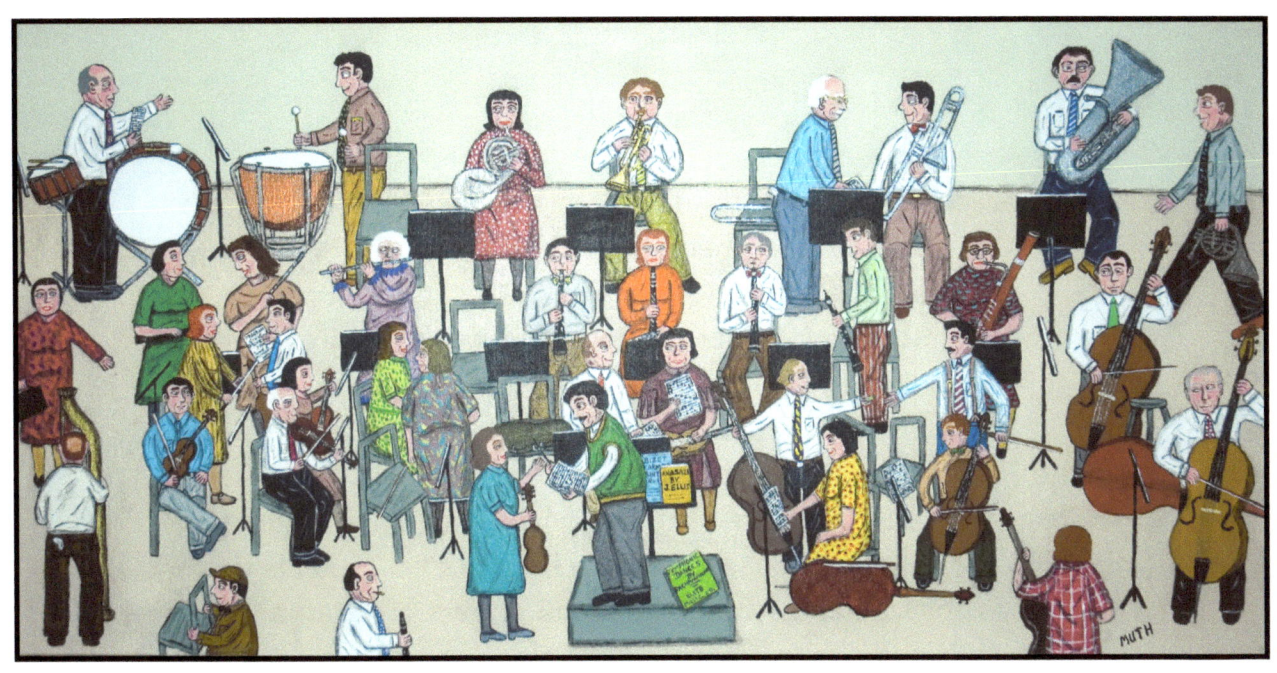

Rehearsal Time, 2001, acrylic on canvas, 15 x 30 inches *(Private Collection)*

Parades were important and exciting events in our lives. We went to see them, standing and waiting along the curb, always ready to cheer and to salute when the flag went by. Marching bands set the tone and were usually from area schools or local civic groups. Floats were not elaborate and often were a theme on the bed of a truck. There was always a parade on the Fourth of July and this painting shows a part of the scene. There is the Grand Marshal on his big white horse followed by the high-stepping band leader and the band. Local officials ride by waving to their constituents. The truck shows children and their animals from the Green County 4-H. Along the sidewalk are the spectators and behind them some typical stores and a bank.

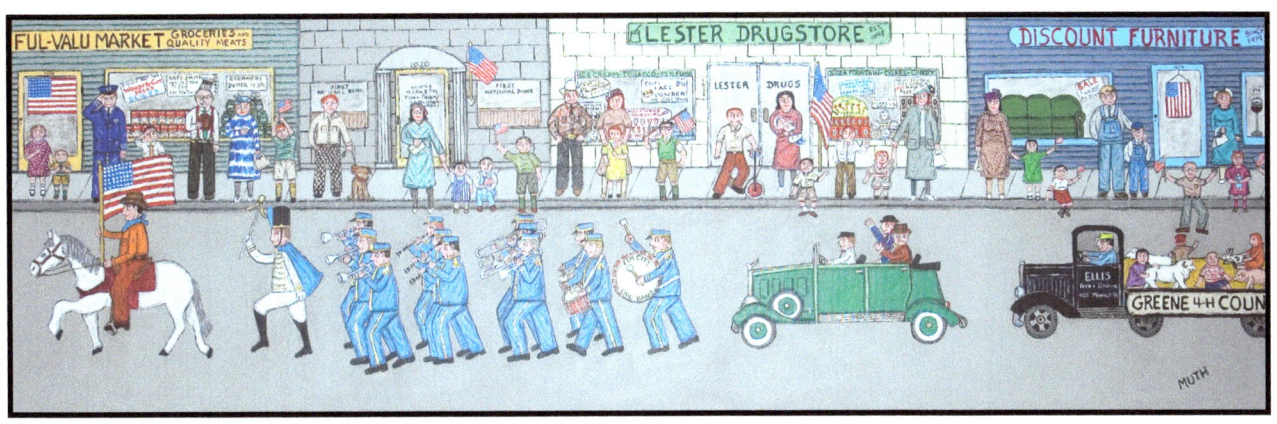

Fourth of July Parade, 2002, acrylic on canvas, 15 x 48 inches
(Private Collection)

The circus parade was one of the most eagerly awaited parades each year. It was a magical transformation of the streets. Suddenly there were elephants, monkeys, exotic wild animals, clowns, giants and midgets. And if in those days you couldn't afford a ticket to the circus performance, you could at least see the free parade. Mulkie's is obviously a first-class three-ring circus with a lot of clowns and animals. In this painting we see spectators on both sides of the street, including an enterprising balloon salesman.

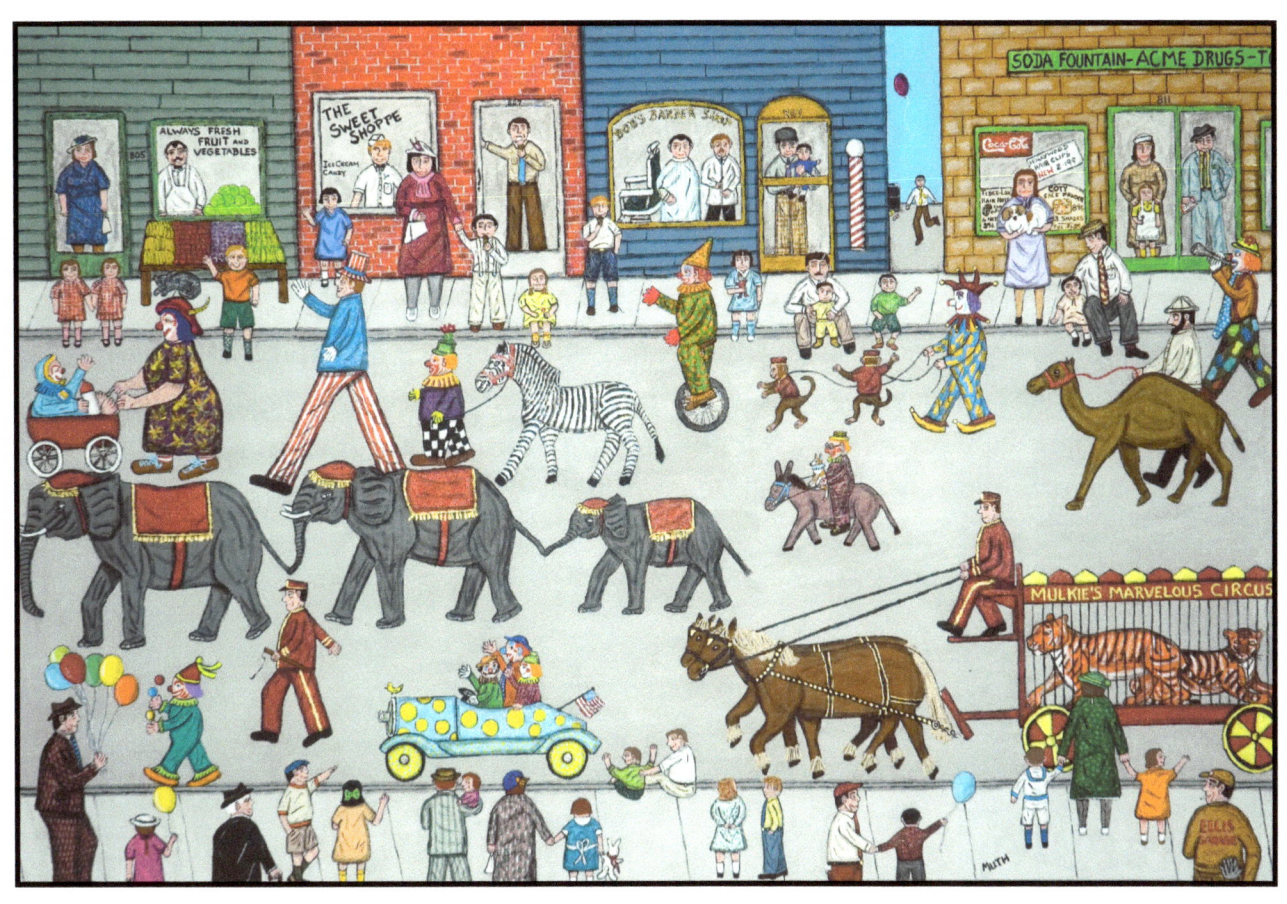

Mulkie's Marvelous Circus, 1998, acrylic on canvas, 24 x 36 inches
(Collection of Marilyn Fisher and Willard Chilcott)

Joddy's is a small circus but with a band, some clowns and at least one elephant. It is going past a block of apartment buildings. It can be assumed that the parade is an unexpected event and treat. One woman has been drying the dishes, another has been vacuuming while one lady continues to do her ironing while watching the parade go past. I've always felt a special affection for the small, less affluent circuses.

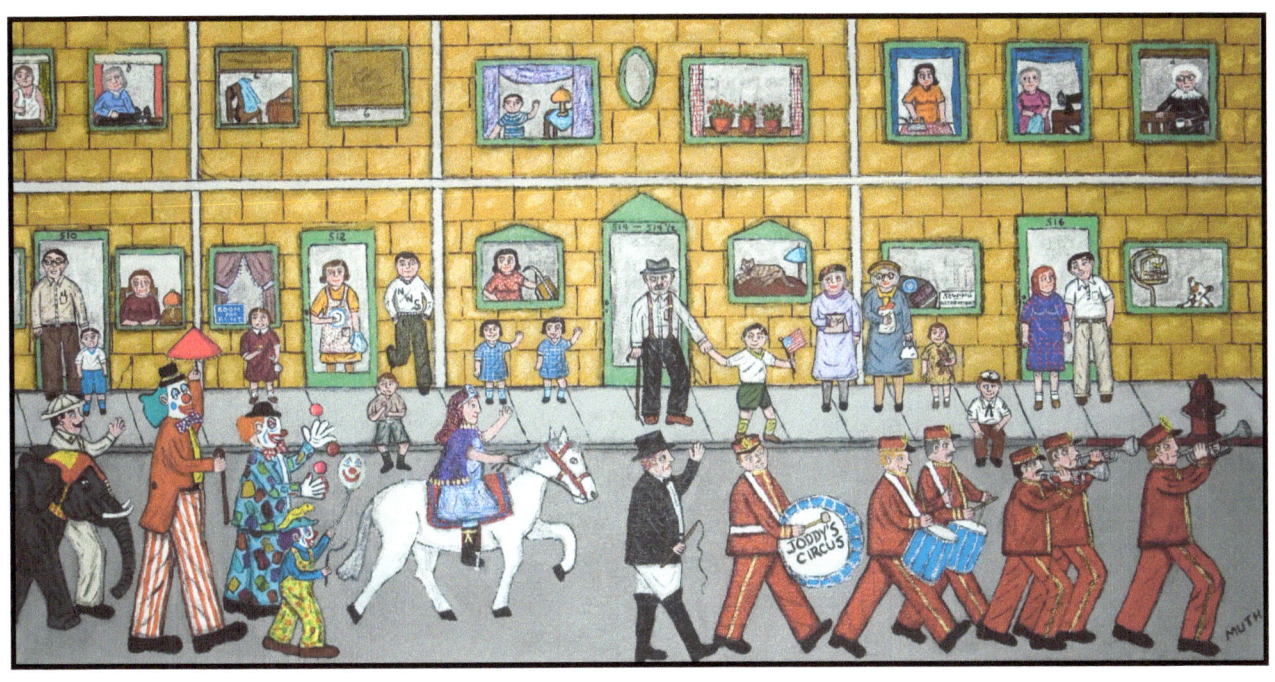

Joddy's Circus Comes To Town, 2004, acrylic on canvas, 15 x 30 inches
(Private Collection)

Who can resist a bakery? The smell of bread, cakes, pies, doughnuts and rolls is intoxicating. While bread could be bought at groceries during the thirties, small bakeries flourished. They offered a wider variety of breads and rolls. Since they were small and family-owned, the goods all tasted homemade. Many bakers had come from Europe and specialized in old country recipes.

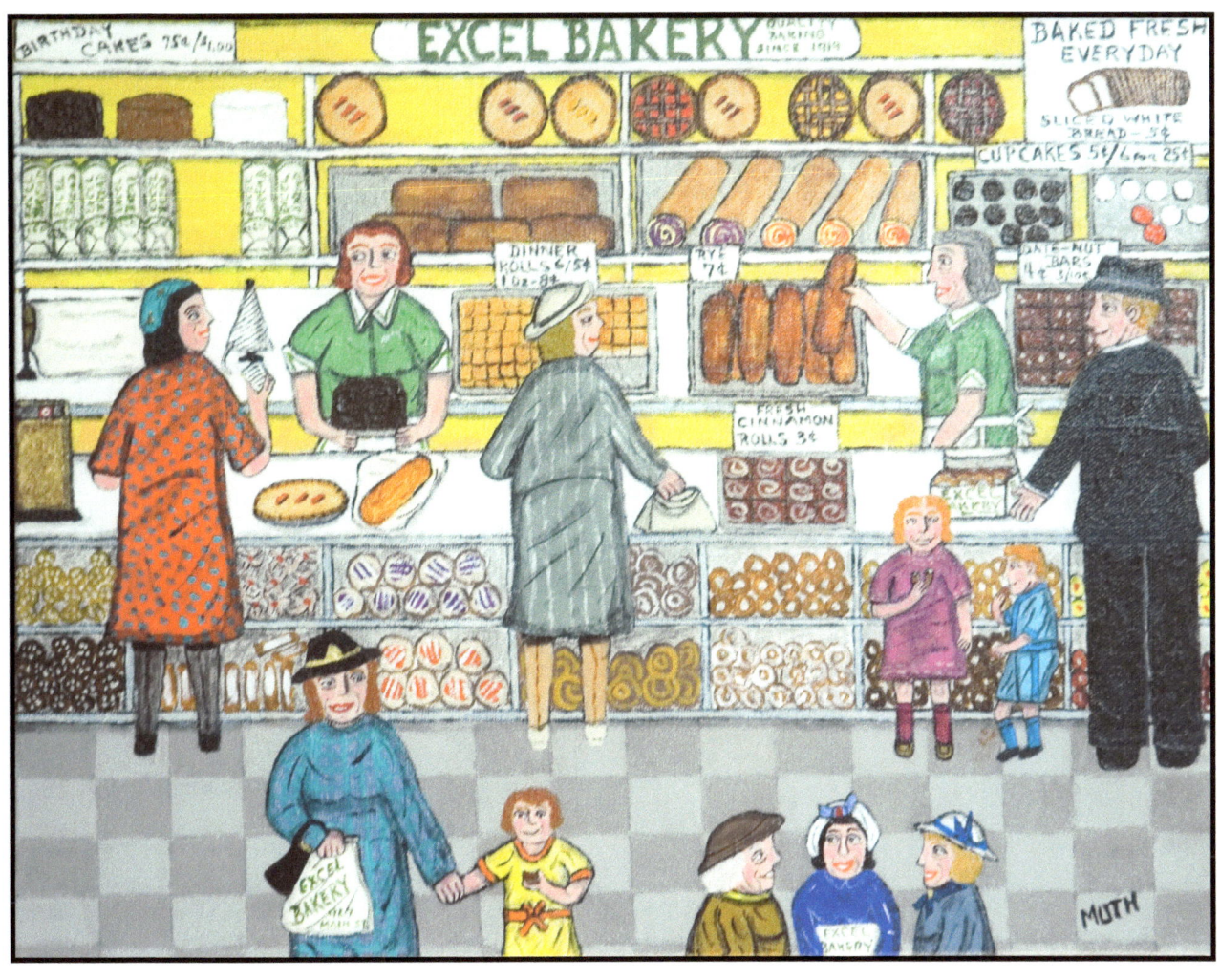

Excel Bakery, 2004, acrylic on canvas, 12 x 16 inches *(Private Collection)*

This a typical afternoon social event in the thirties. It is an outdoor tea party and in this painting it is an autograph party. The author is seated at a small table at the left. The tea table with its refreshments is at the back and next to it a trio is playing appropriate music. All the women are dressed in their best and are wearing hats and some have gloves. When working on the painting I felt that the party was given by a women's club, possibly a book club. As I often have done, a cat is included, a keen observer of the scene.

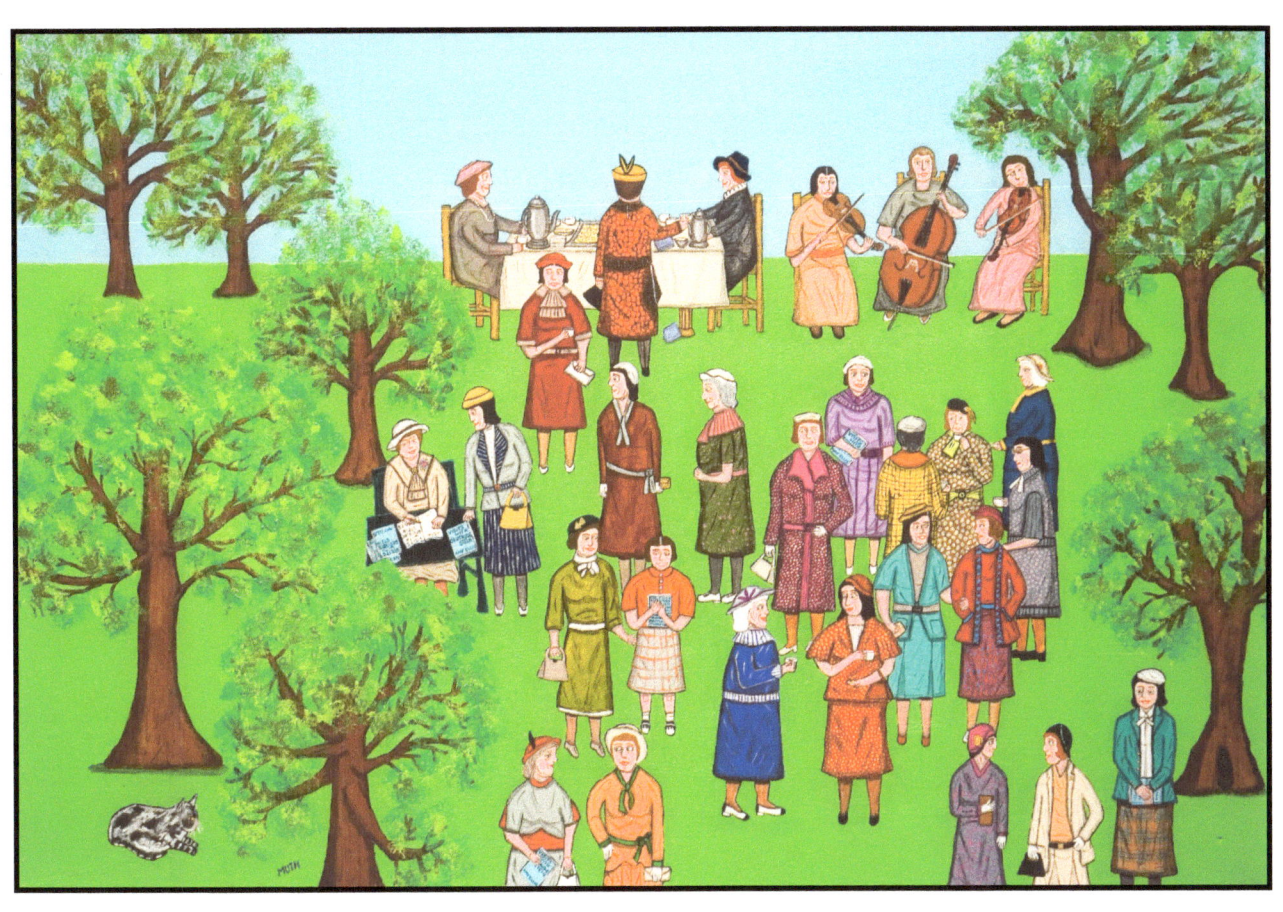

The Garden Party, 1991, acrylic on canvas, 24 x 36 inches
(Collection of Dr. Gail Kaplan and Sondra Everhart)

"Vacation" in the thirties meant "going to the lake" if you lived anywhere near water. In Indiana it meant going to one of the lakes like Lake James and staying for a week or two in a rented cottage. Near Buffalo, New York we went over to Crystal Beach in Canada where you could stay in a cottage or in a boarding house where you could also get your meals. Cottages had the barest amenities and usually a collection of mismatched furniture. None of that mattered, however, for the most important thing was the "beach." Children played in the sand and in the water. Adults would swim or float or just sit on the sand. It was a time for relaxing, reading, eating snacks and daydreaming. It took us, children and adults, outside our usual routines. It was a time of exploration and to us the lake was a mighty ocean of possibilities.

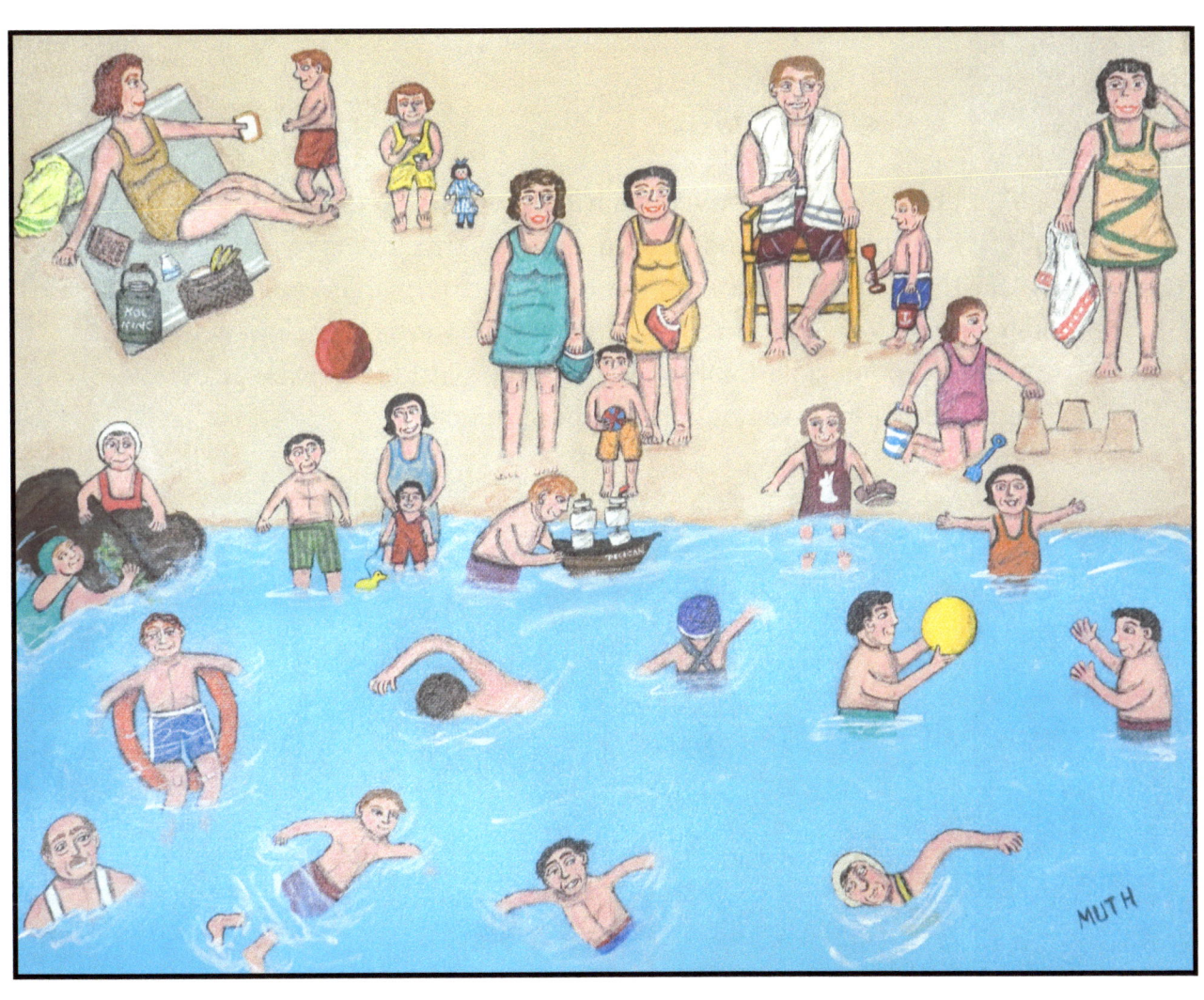

Rye Beach, 2000, acrylic on canvas, 14 x 18 inches (Private Collection)

Although I have never seen clowns rehearse, this is what I imagine happens. There are eleven clowns working on their acts. There are two dogs and two monkeys. One is riding a unicycle, another is juggling and one is dancing with a life-size wooden doll. Each clown is busy with his particular part. There is an air of anticipation and confidence.

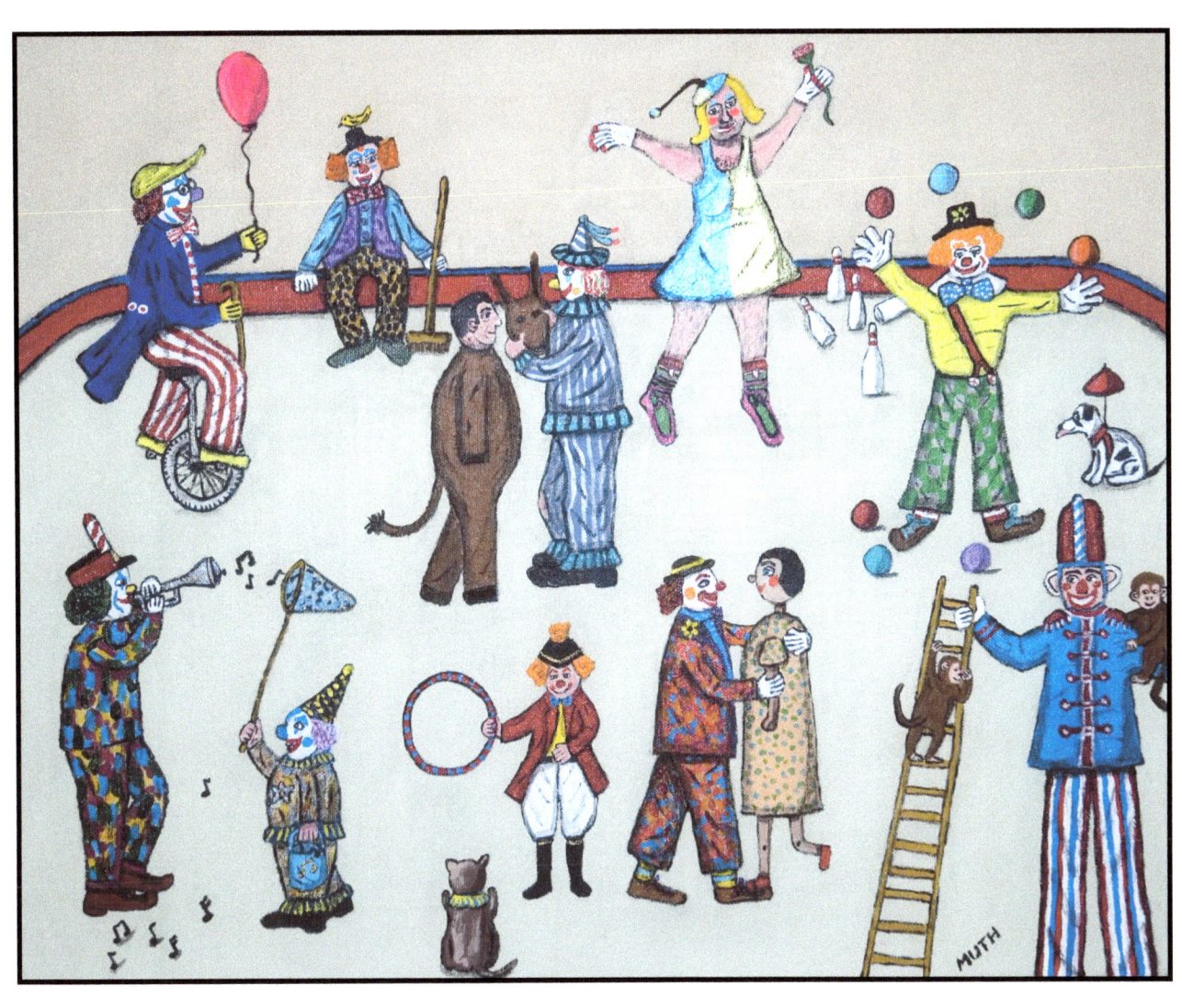

The Clowns Rehearse, 2005, acrylic on canvas, 16 x 20 inches
(Collection of the Artist)

The owner of this painting is an ardent biker. He decided it would be fun to have his own bike shop. There are both adults and children. Repair work is being done. One couple are having their lunch. In those days the bicycles were heavy and "thick." Flat tires were a common problem. There is a boy on a scooter and two boys with a homemade car. As usual several dogs have joined the fun and there is even a cat up a tree looking over the whole scene. No one seems to be in a hurry; it's a pleasant afternoon.

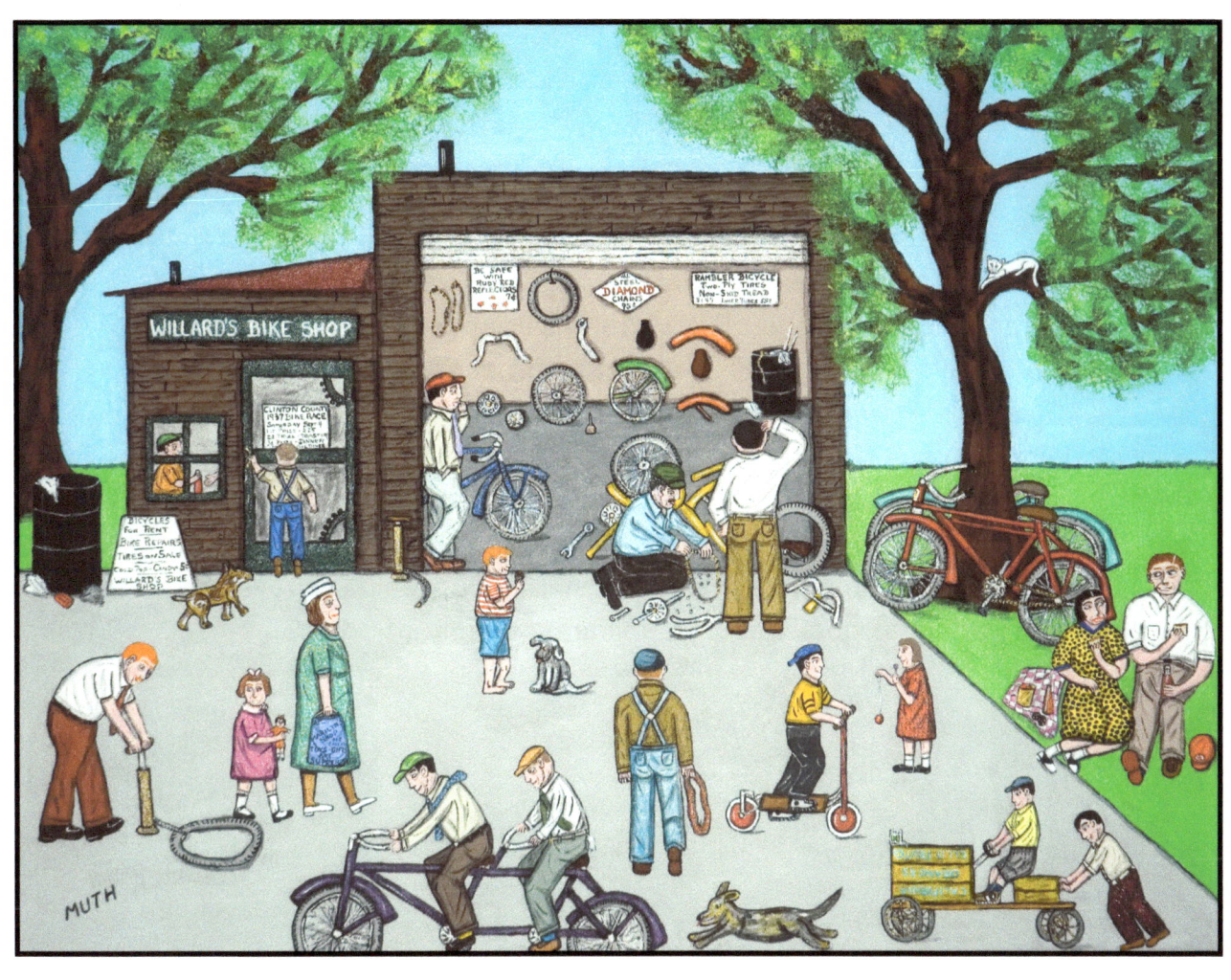

Willard's Bike Shop, 1993, acrylic on canvas, 18 x 24 inches
(Collection of Marilyn Fisher and Willard Chilcott)

This is a typical small town hardware store where the owner and clerks knew where everything was and how it should be used. The hardware store was also a neighborhood center. The owner and clerks knew everyone who came in. They also always knew just what a customer needed despite the some-times vague descriptions. This was the store where you went for paint, tools and plumbing supplies. They also carried household items—brooms, teakettles, coffee pots and roasting pans. In this painting it is obviously spring as a man and his son are leaving the store with a wheelbarrow and gardening supplies. It always had a wide variety of goods and an unlimited supply of advice.

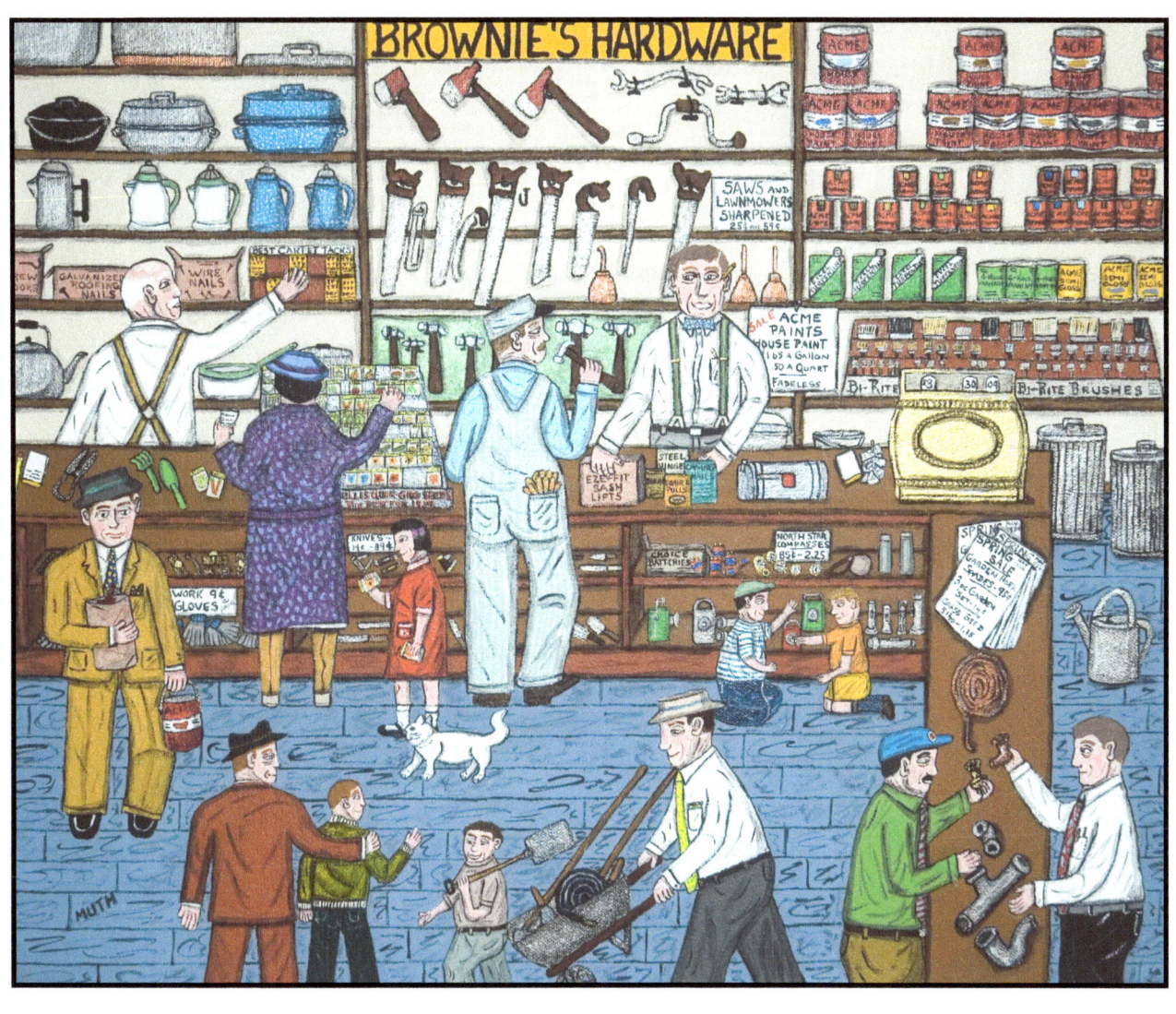

Brownie's Hardware, 1993, acrylic on canvas, 16 x 20 inches
(Collection of Marilyn Fisher and Willard Chilcott)

The toy business was not the big business it is today. Most toys were sold in the dime stores or large department stores. Advertising was at a minimum. Mail order catalogs always included a few pages of toys. In some large cities, a toy store similar to the one in this painting could be found. It was customary to offer layaways for larger purchases. In those days before credit cards, a person could pick out a big ticket item, pay something down and the store would put it away and hold until the final payment was made. This shop has a variety of the most popular toys. There are dolls, stuffed animals, doll houses, games, toy cars and trains. Parcheesi and checkers were popular games. There was a definite gender distinction at the time—boys got chemistry sets, Lincoln Logs, Erector sets and cars. Girls, in addition to dolls and their outfits, got play dishes, pots and pans and toy ironing boards. The most expensive items shown in the painting are the pedal cars, wagon and doll buggies. In those days between the wars some of the most popular items were toy soldiers and toy guns.

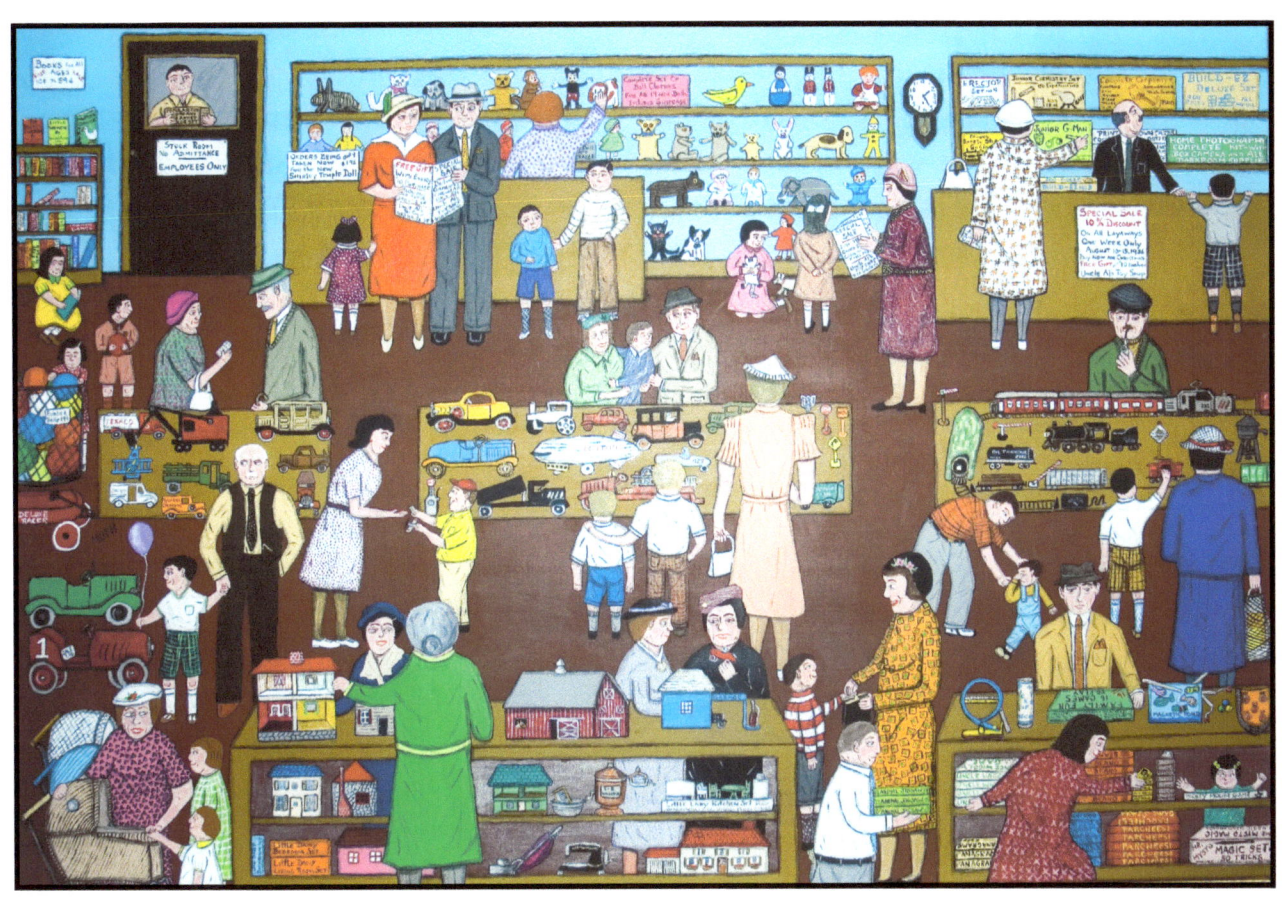

Uncle Al's Toy Shop, 1987, acrylic on canvas, 24 x 36 inches
(Private Collection)

Of all the stores that used to exist and have since disappeared, the one I miss the most was the Dime Store or as some people called it "the Five and Ten." Unlike the other stores I have written about, these were big, company stores and in some areas more known by their corporate names. The two major ones were Woolworth and Kresge's. An early Kresge catalog from 1913 shows that they did indeed start out with merchandise priced at five and ten cents. By the time of the thirties while you could still get some items for five or ten cents, you found a lot at slightly higher prices. It was the variety that attracted customers. In a large Woolworth, you could find almost anything you wanted plus many other things you didn't know you needed. It was the place to shop for household products from pots and pans to dish towels and table cloths. You could buy canaries, fish and little turtles. Some stores had a special section of sheet music with a lady who would play your selections for you to help you decide if you wanted it or not. Most of the large stores had lunch counters as can be seen in the painting. Their food was good and cheap. They were very popular with people who worked in the area. Their menus and price were similar to that offered in diners. The lunch counter was also a popular place for shoppers to stay and have a dish of ice cream or a soda in the middle of the afternoon. There were toys, stationery, silverware and lots of fancy imported geegaws. It was a shopper's paradise and every counter had one or two clerks eager to wait on you.

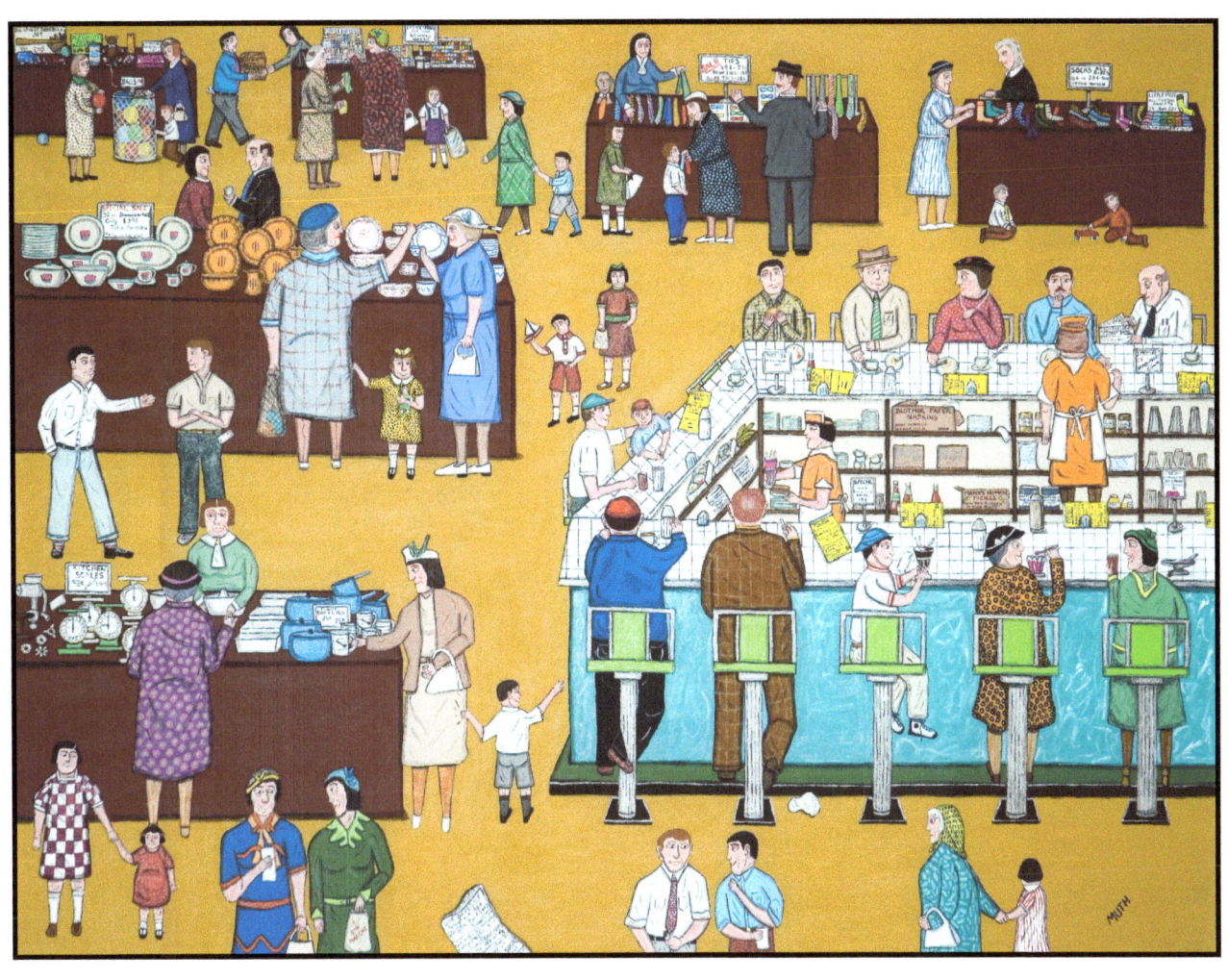

Dime Store, 1992, acrylic on canvas, 36 x 48 inches
(Collection of Dr. Gail Kaplan and Sondra Everhart)

This is a scene from a circus. The audience of adults and children are enthralled by the trapeze artists except for one little boy who is frightened and fearful to look. His mother is trying to reassure him. His fears are groundless for they are experts and in any case there is a safety net.

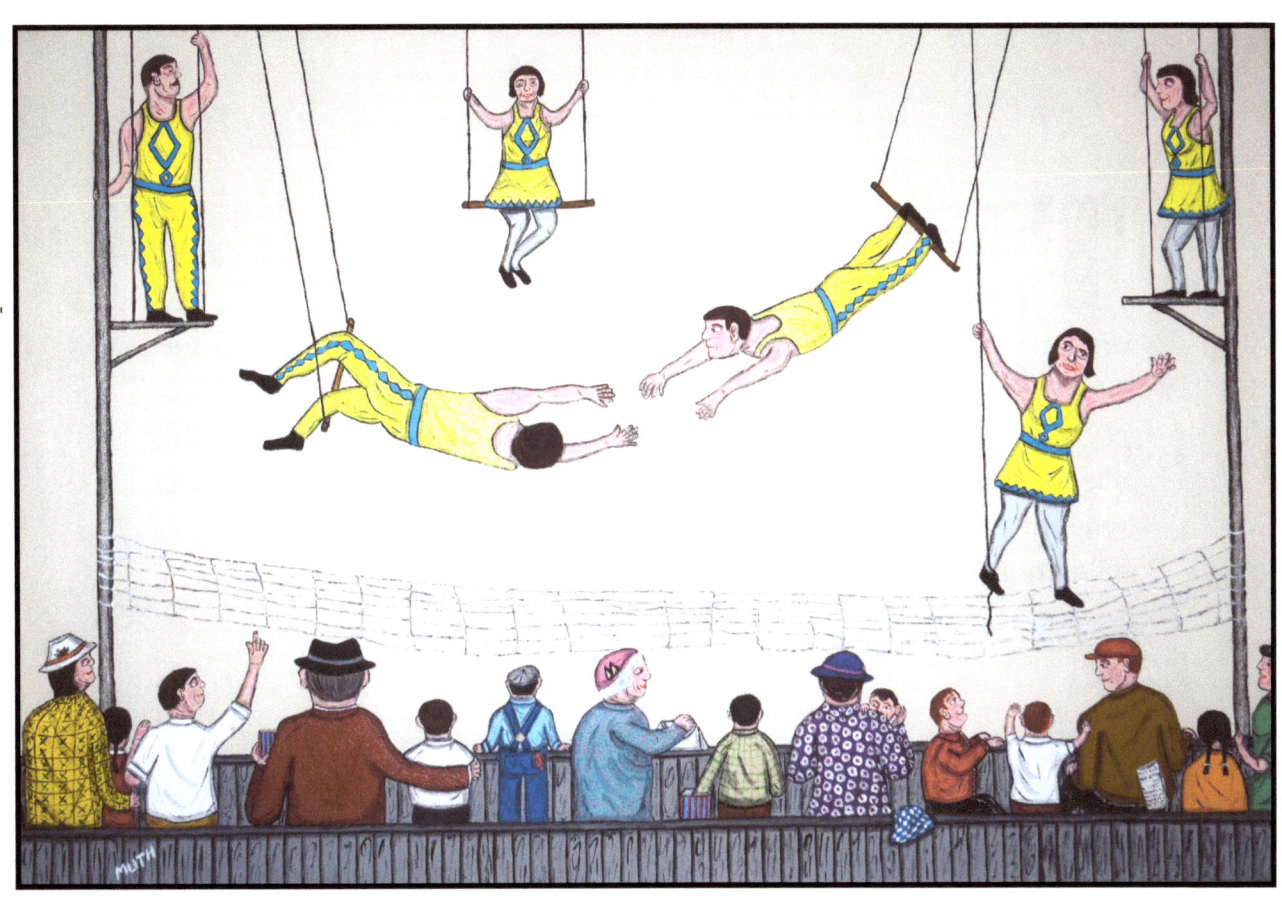

Flying High, 1989, acrylic on canvas, 24 x 36 inches *(Collection of the Artist)*

This is a street scene with a small but busy diner as the center of attention. We see only a part of a large building on one side and a part of one window of an auto parts store on the other side. There are the usual busy adults and children. A satisfied customer has left the Acme Auto Parts with his purchase. A boy is eating an ice cream cone. You can look down the alley and see a dog sniffing at the garbage cans. One customer is waving from the diner window—that must be his friend, a fellow salesman, coming to join him.

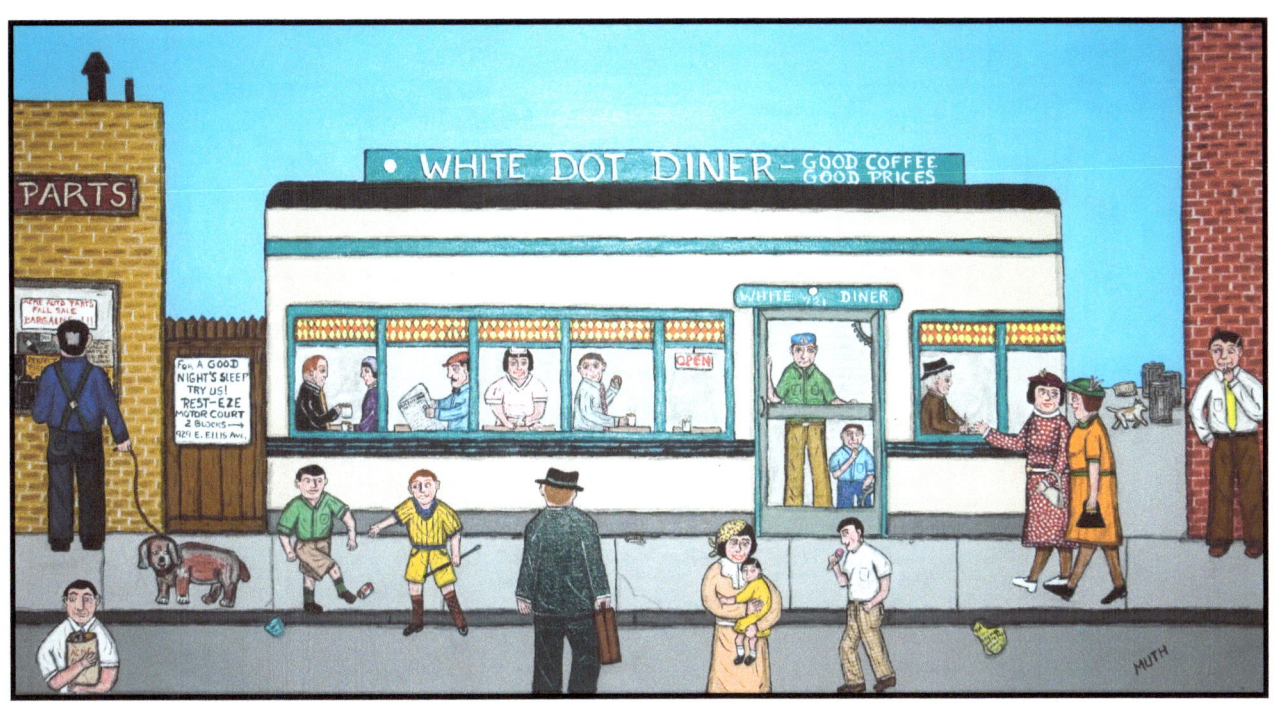

White Dot Diner, 1990, acrylic on canvas, 16 x 36 inches
(Collection of Marilyn Fisher and Willard Chilcott)

Political rallies have always been a part of the election process. It is a way for candidates to get to know their constituents and also persuade uncertain voters to support them. Back in the thirties, particularly in small towns and rural areas, these rallies were rather simple affairs. Two things guaranteed good attendance—a dance and food. In the painting the party or the candidate has hired a Grange hall and a small lively band. On the right side of the painting are tables with homemade pies, cakes and cookies. There is coffee and lemonade. The candidate is passing out leaflets and at some point, we know he will take the stage and give a speech.

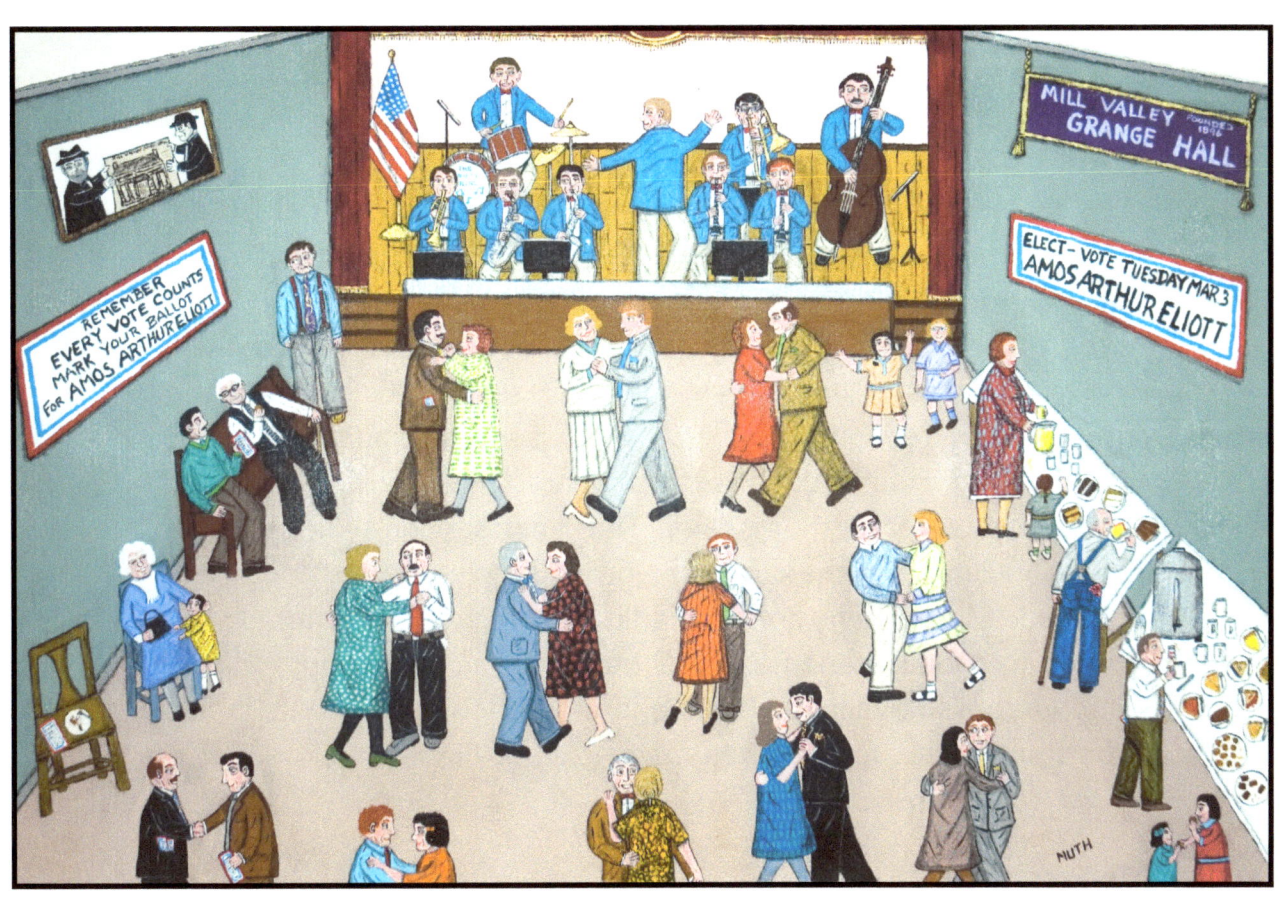

The Rally, 2004, acrylic on canvas, 24 x 36 inches *(Collection of the Artist)*

Diners were once among the most popular places to eat. They were very accessible, had good food and cheap prices. The owner was usually also the cook. The food was not fancy or elaborate. In fact, most diners prided themselves on having "home style food." Desserts which cost five or ten cents were limited to pies, cakes, jello and pudding. Donuts, hamburgers and hot dogs were standard fare. There were no fast food restaurants in those days. The diner service was quick and friendly. Sitting at the counter, you could watch your food being cooked. Music came from a radio on the back counter. It was tuned to a local station. Coffee was the main drink, but milk and pop were also available. Black and white floors were popular and the front of the counter was marbleized or tiled.

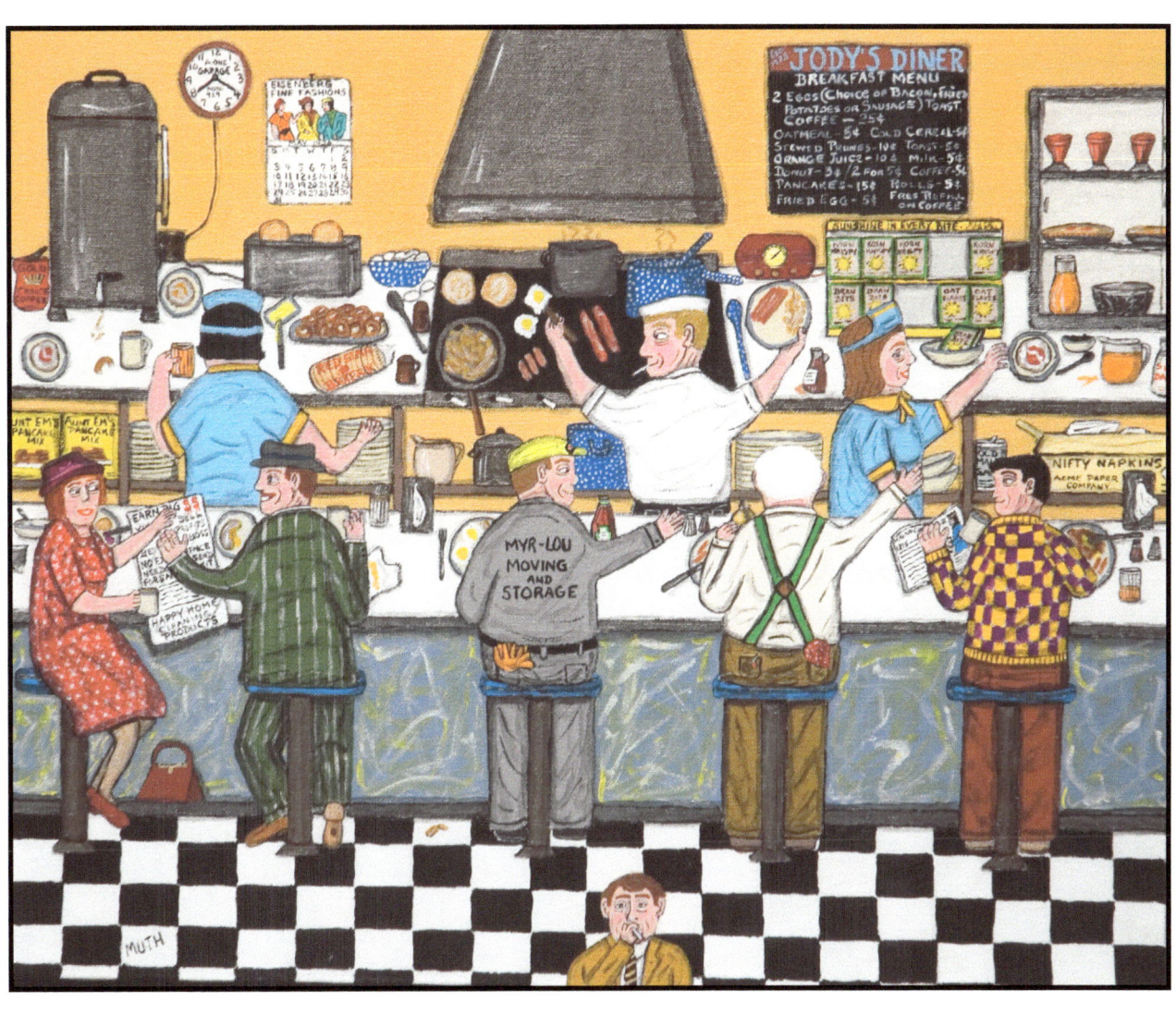

Jody's Diner, 1996, acrylic on canvas, 16 x 20 inches
(Collection of Dr. Gail Kaplan and Sondra Everhart)

Some diners were large enough that in addition to the counter, they had booths. They were especially prized by couples. However, as this painting shows, there was no privacy from young children who were in an adjacent booth. As expected there is a variety of customers enjoying the food.

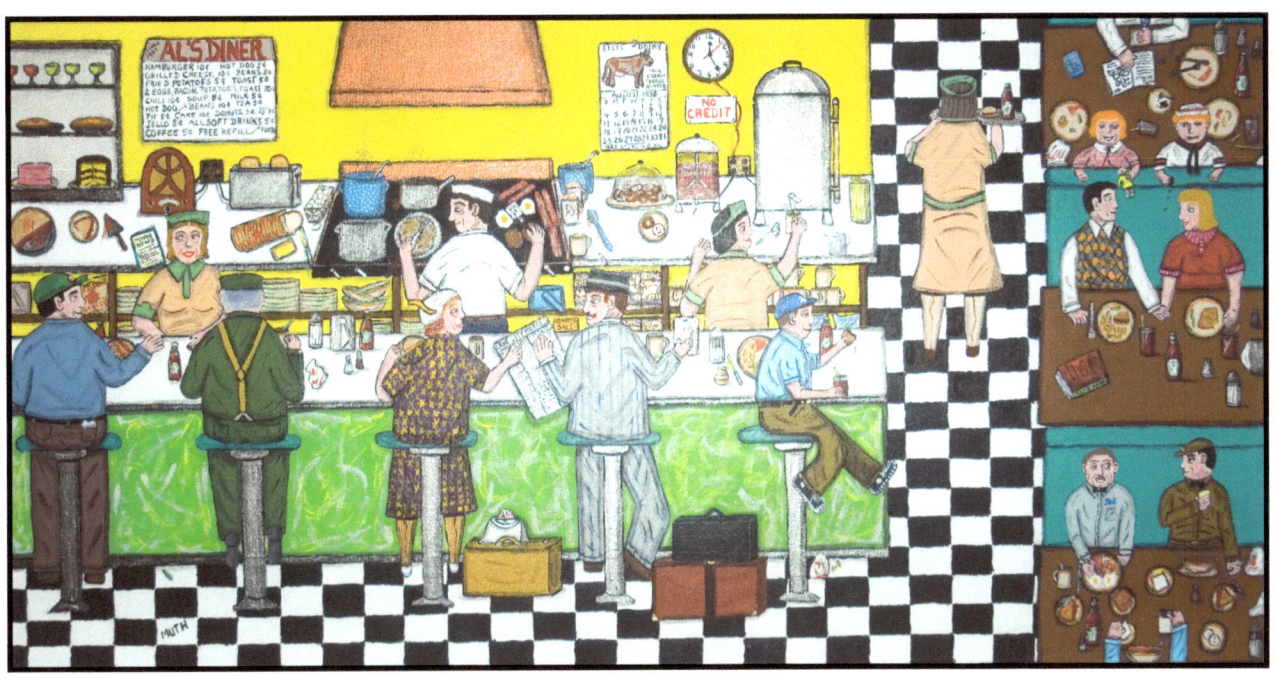

Al's Diner, 1995, acrylic on canvas, 15 x 30 inches *(Private Collection)*

This quiet street scene with shops closed and shades drawn is my tribute to Edward Hopper's painting *Early Sunday Morning.*

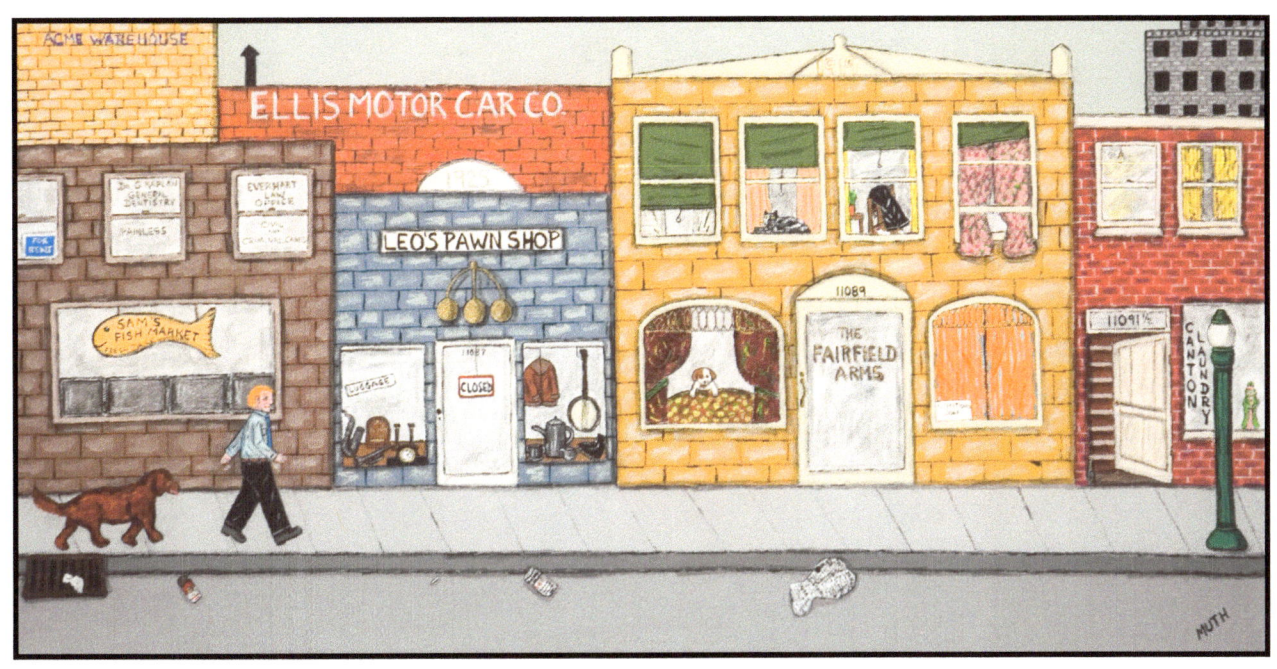

Edwardsville, 1997, acrylic on canvas, 15 x 30 inches
(Collection of Dr. Gail Kaplan and Sondra Everhart)

Clowns and children have a relationship that is both dichotomous and age-old. It is one of joy, sometimes fear, doubt and fascination. Some children give shrieks of joy when approached by a clown while others cry in terror and seek the safety and solace of adults. In this painting two children are at ease with the clown while the two children in the background are not sure if they want to come closer or not.

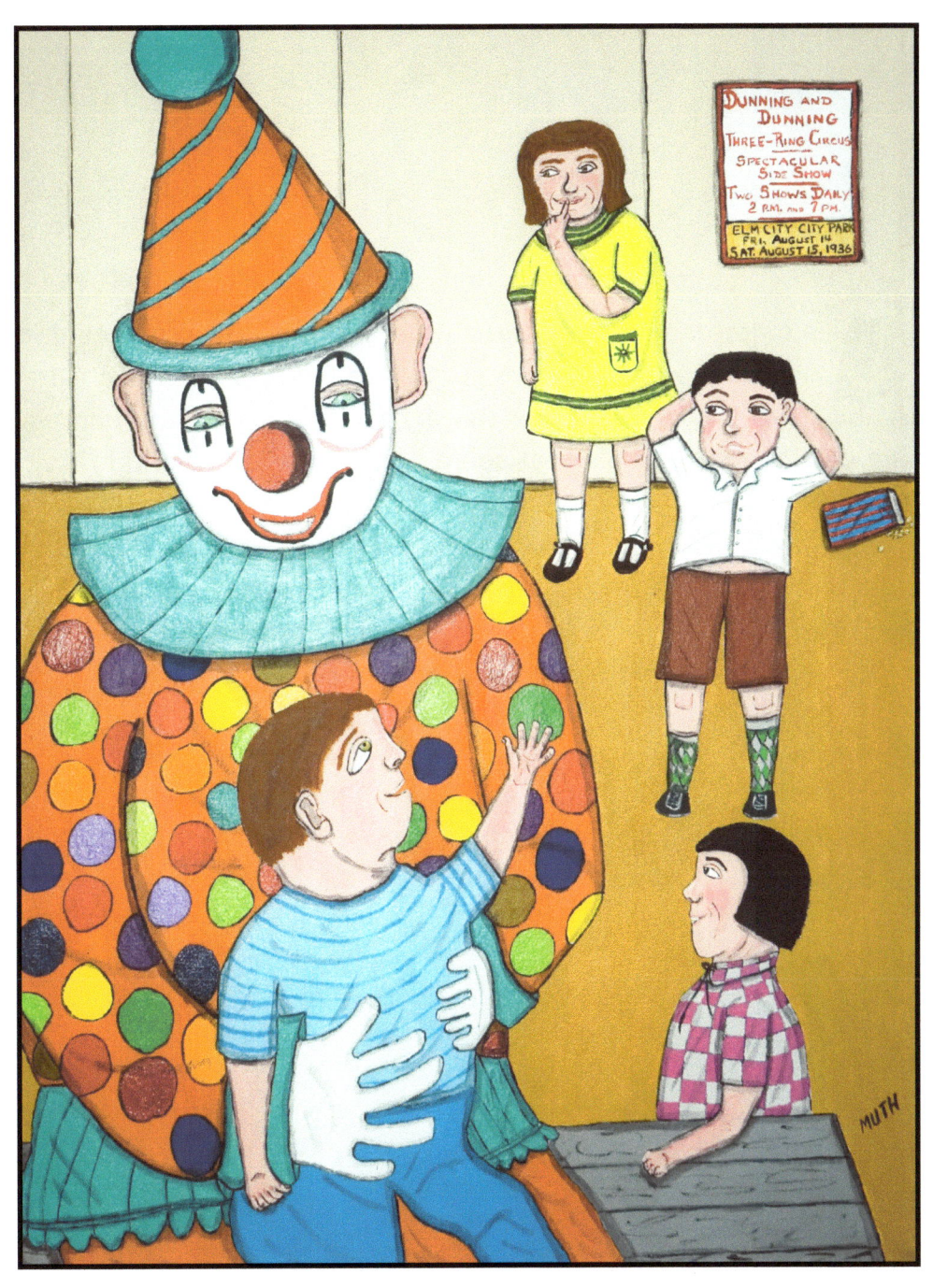

Rudi the Clown, 1989, acrylic on canvas, 24 x 18 inches
(Collection of the Artist)

An entrepreneur has set up a Merry-go-Round in a vacant lot next to a pasture where horses are being kept. The children have a chance to ride the exotic animals on the carousel and pet the real animals that seem eager for their attention.

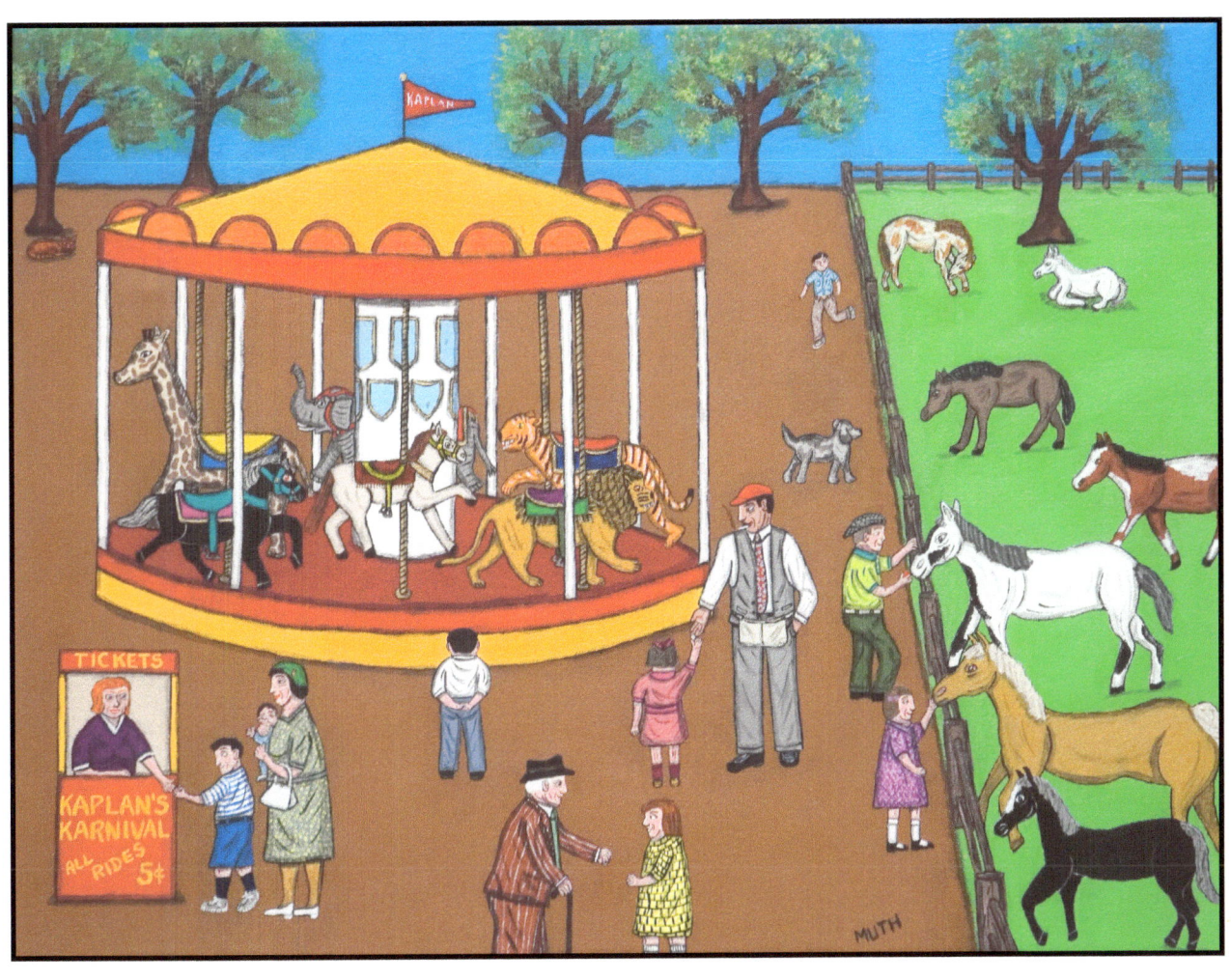

Carousel, 1993, acrylic on canvas, 18 x 24 inches
(Collection of Dr. Gail Kaplan and Sondra Everhart)

Although this is a rather small show the owners and their dogs are just as serious as if it were the Westminster show. It is the end of the show and proud owners are being presented with a Best of Show trophy. Other owners with their pets are mulling over the results of the show. Naturally, every person thinks his or her pet is the best. One woman seems to be arguing this point with one of the judges. A white cat in the tree is watching the scene with amused detachment.

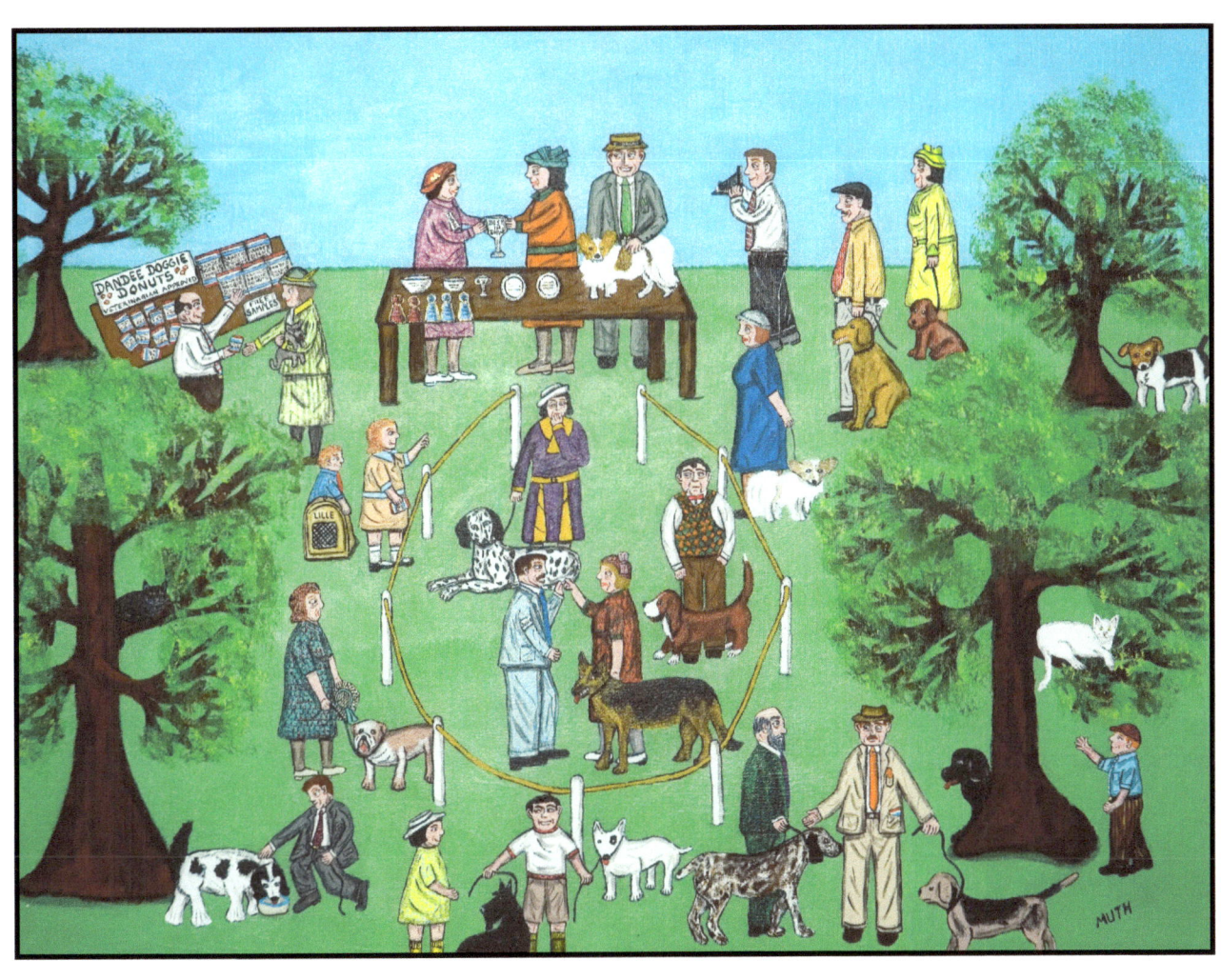

Dog Show, 1997, acrylic on canvas, 18 x 24 inches
(Collection of Marilyn Fisher and Willard Chilcott)

Unlike the diners, this is a really fancy restaurant. The food is excellent and the service impeccable. The desserts are fancy as we can see from the one table being served house specialties. This being the thirties, a dinner might cost as much as three or four dollars. Why the name Lake Como? I thought it sounded grand and fit the place.

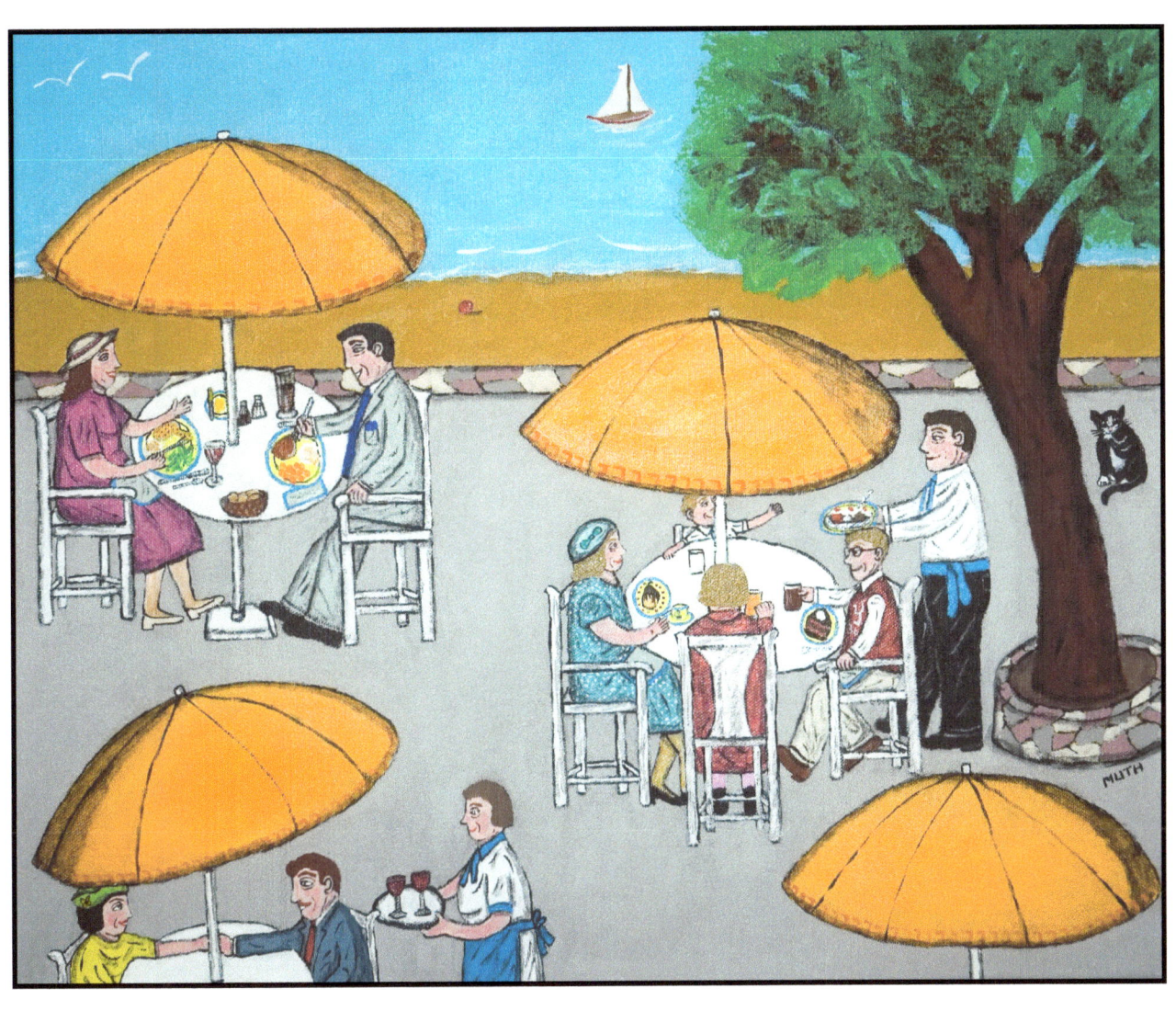

The Restaurant at Lake Como, 2005, acrylic on canvas, 16 x 20 inches
(Collection of the Artist)

This is a different view of the traditional diner. This time we are facing the chef and the diners. We are inside and look out the windows to the world outside. We have a good view of the front and back counters.

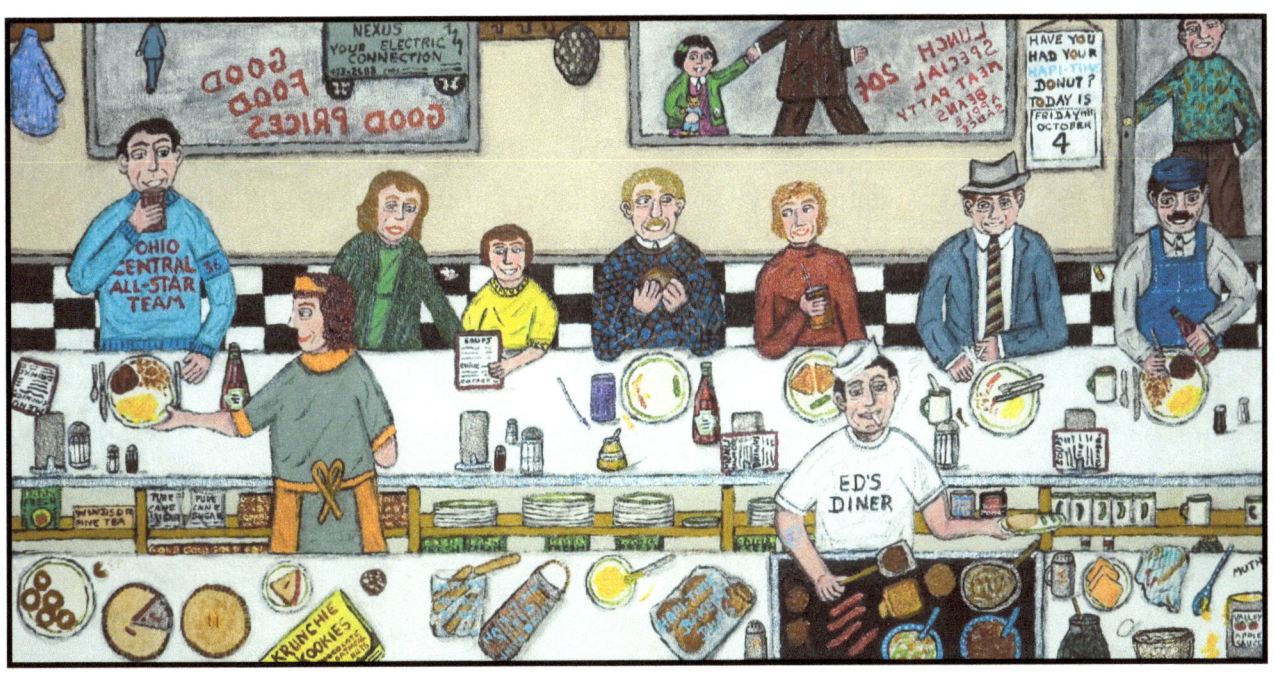

Lunch Counter, 2006, acrylic on canvas, 12 x 24 inches
(Galerie Bonheur; www.galeriebonheur.com)

Although electricity revolutionized factory methods, many workers were still required. Most of the machinery required "hands-on" or at least close supervision. People took pride in their work. They were an integral part of the manufacturing process.

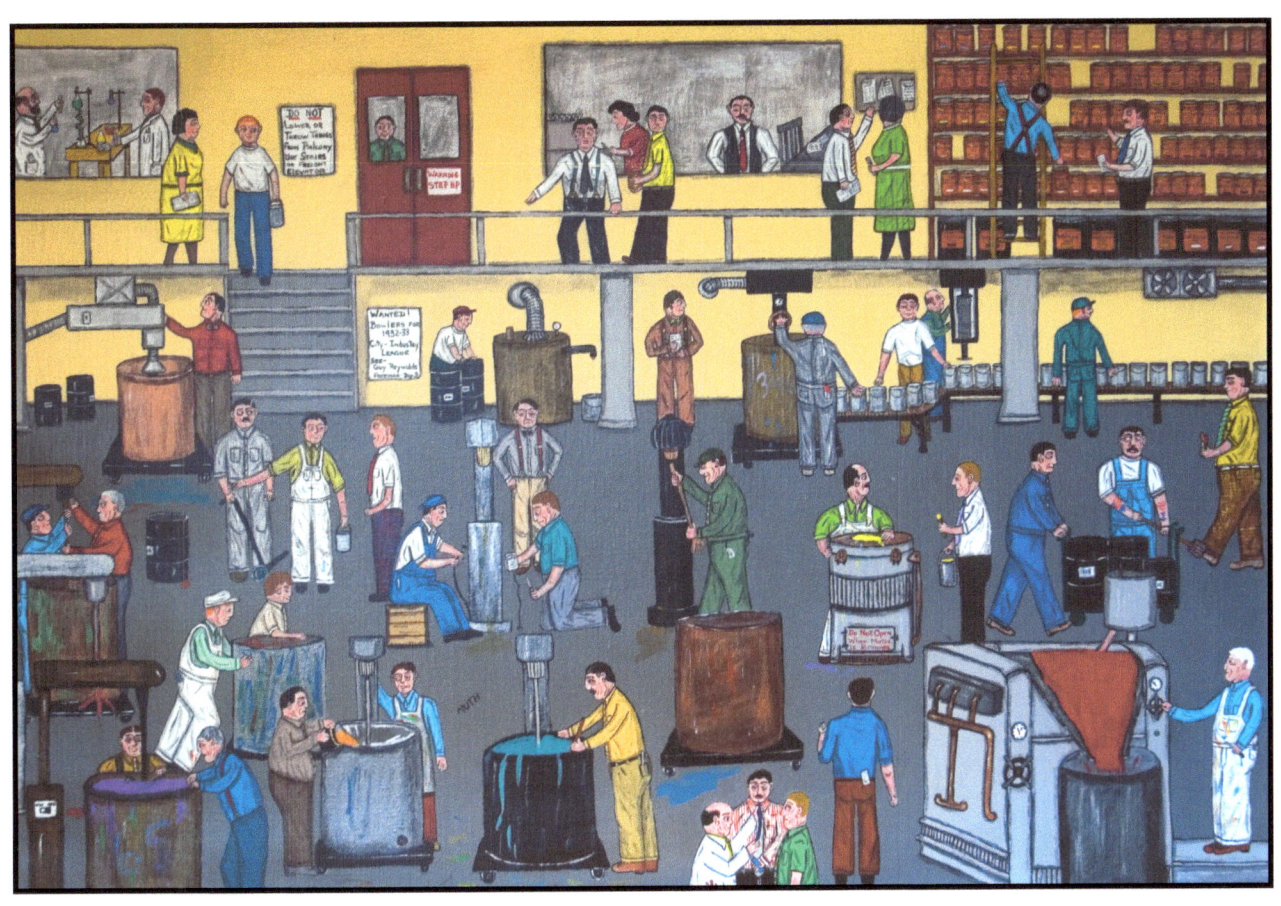

The Paint Factory, 1985, acrylic on canvas, 24 x 36 inches *(Private Collection)*

One of the most exciting events in town was when a carnival came to town. The Midway was where the games of chance were, the food booths and the rides. Sometimes there were fortunetellers. It always seemed like a place of magic and mystery. As children we did not see beyond the surface glitter.

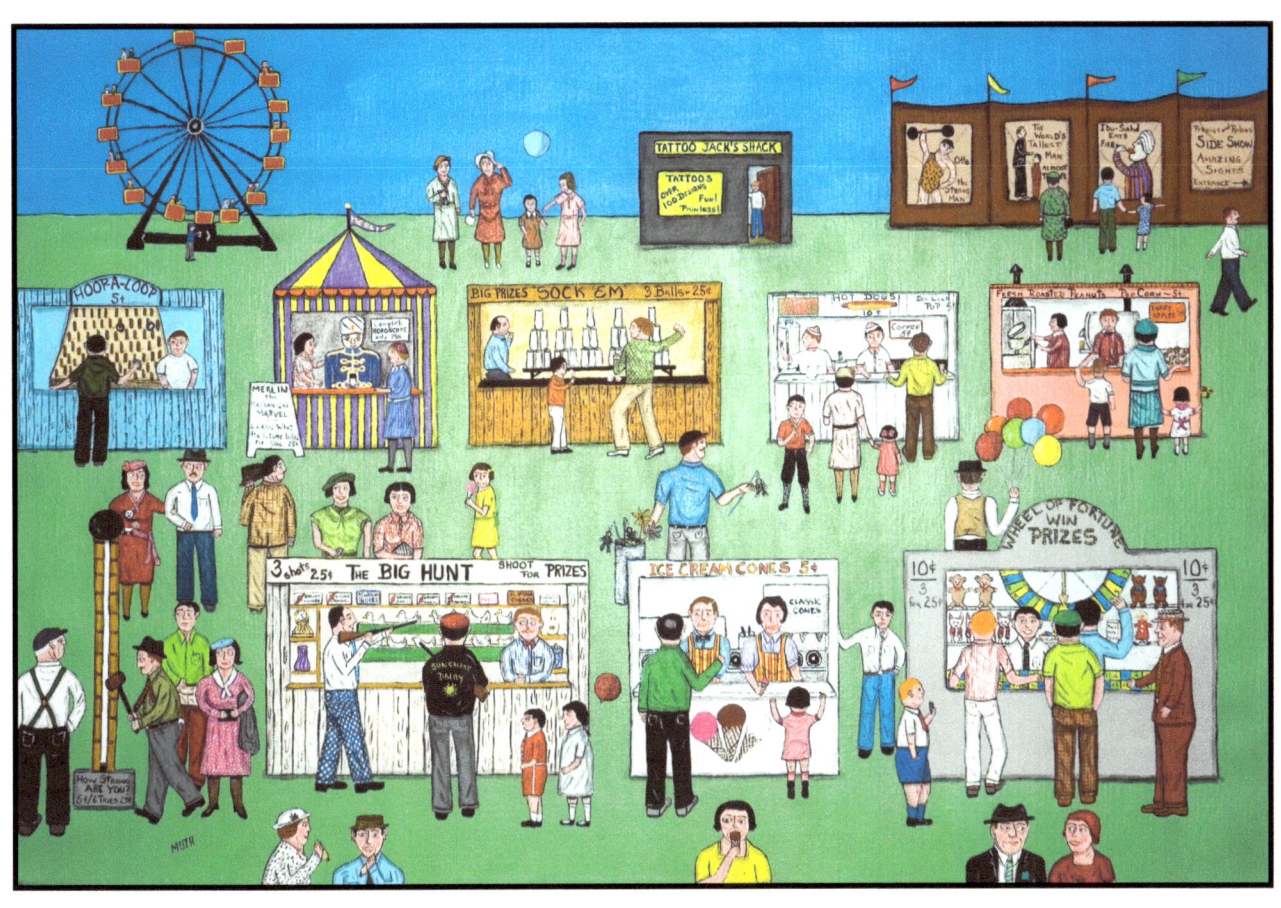

Midway, 1984, acrylic on canvas, 24 x 36 inches
(Collection of Marilyn Fisher and Willard Chilcott)

Street life was always busy even in a residential area. There were salesmen with their sample cases going door to door taking orders for household products or trying to sell insurance. Delivery wagons came from nearby bakeries, groceries and department stores. Hucksters sold fruit and other produce. People were not in a hurry. They took time to stop and chat. As can be seen in this painting, people inside the houses also kept a sharp eye on what was going on in the street.

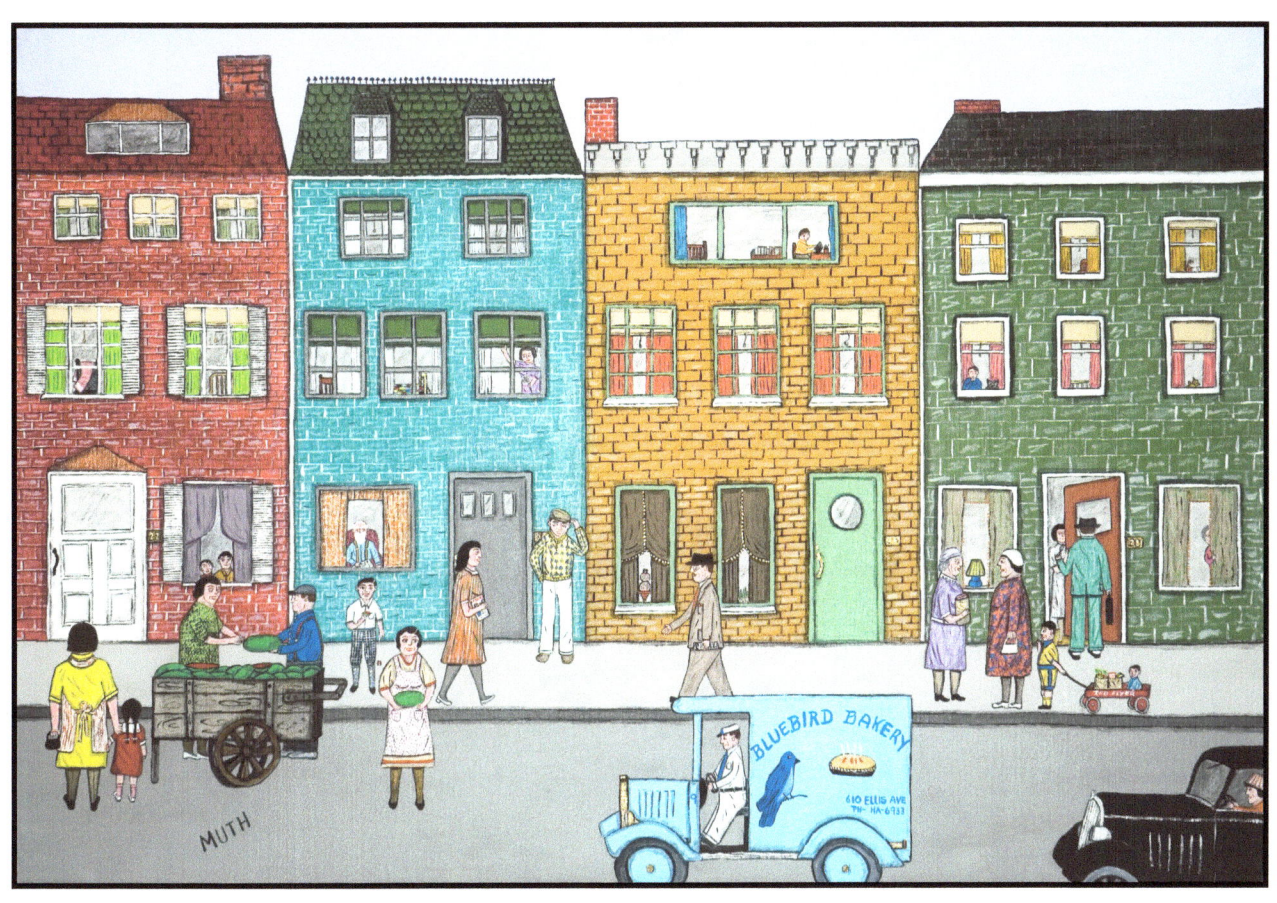

Pintor Place, 1985, acrylic on canvas, 24 x 36 inches
(Collection of Marilyn Fisher and Willard Chilcott)

In the thirties you often saw nuns dressed in their distinctive habits. No matter what your religious affiliation, you always felt a sense of respect toward them. Also sometimes a sense of awe for here were women who had given up their private lives to serve the public good. It was the nuns who were the driving force in the schools, the clinics, orphanages and old age homes.

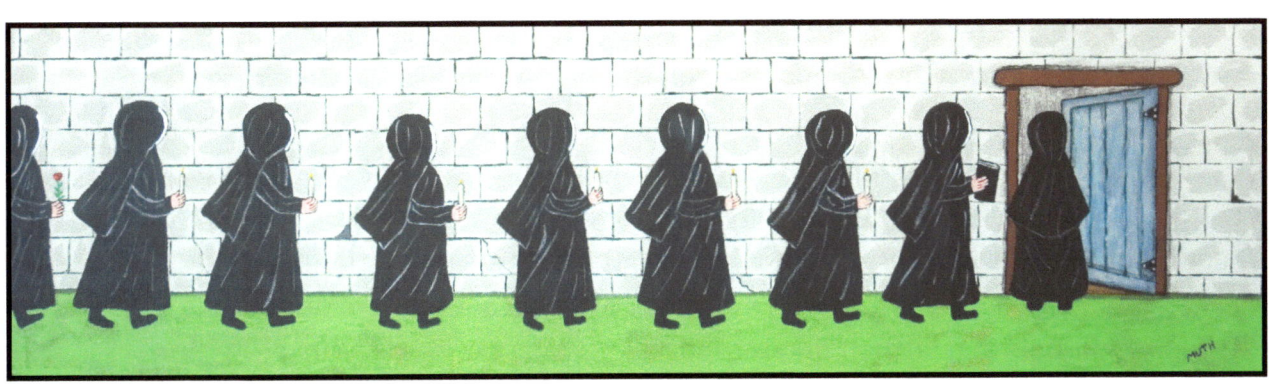

Nuns, 2005, acrylic on canvas, 10 x 36 inches
(Collection of Sylvia Garcia and Family)

There is a real Don Juan's Paint & Body Shop in Santa Fe and it is a popular and thriving business. My painting is what the place would have looked like if it had been there in the thirties. When the owners of the business asked me to do a painting of their shop, they also asked me to visit their place and meet the workers. I went and at the end of my visit, I explained that while it was all very neat and well-arranged, it would make a dull painting. I then suggested that we set it in the thirties, when more work was done by "hands-on" rather than computers. So I went back to the period when the hydraulic lift was considered modern.

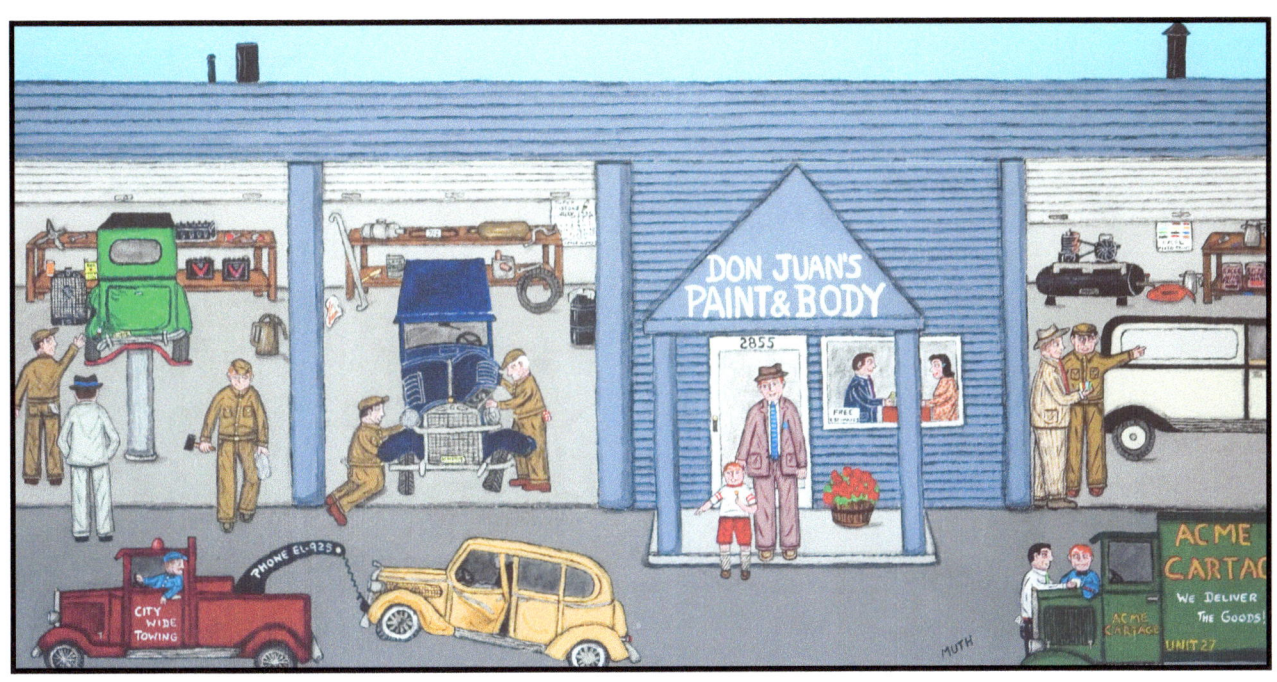

*Don Juan's Paint & Body, 1999, acrylic on canvas, 15 x 30 inches
(Collection of Don Juan's Paint & Body)*

I thought of this lady as a semi-professional fortuneteller who does it for her friends and for her own enjoyment. I feel sure that her fortunes are always "good" ones with promises of happiness and prosperity. To help her in her divinations, she has a crystal ball and an almanac.

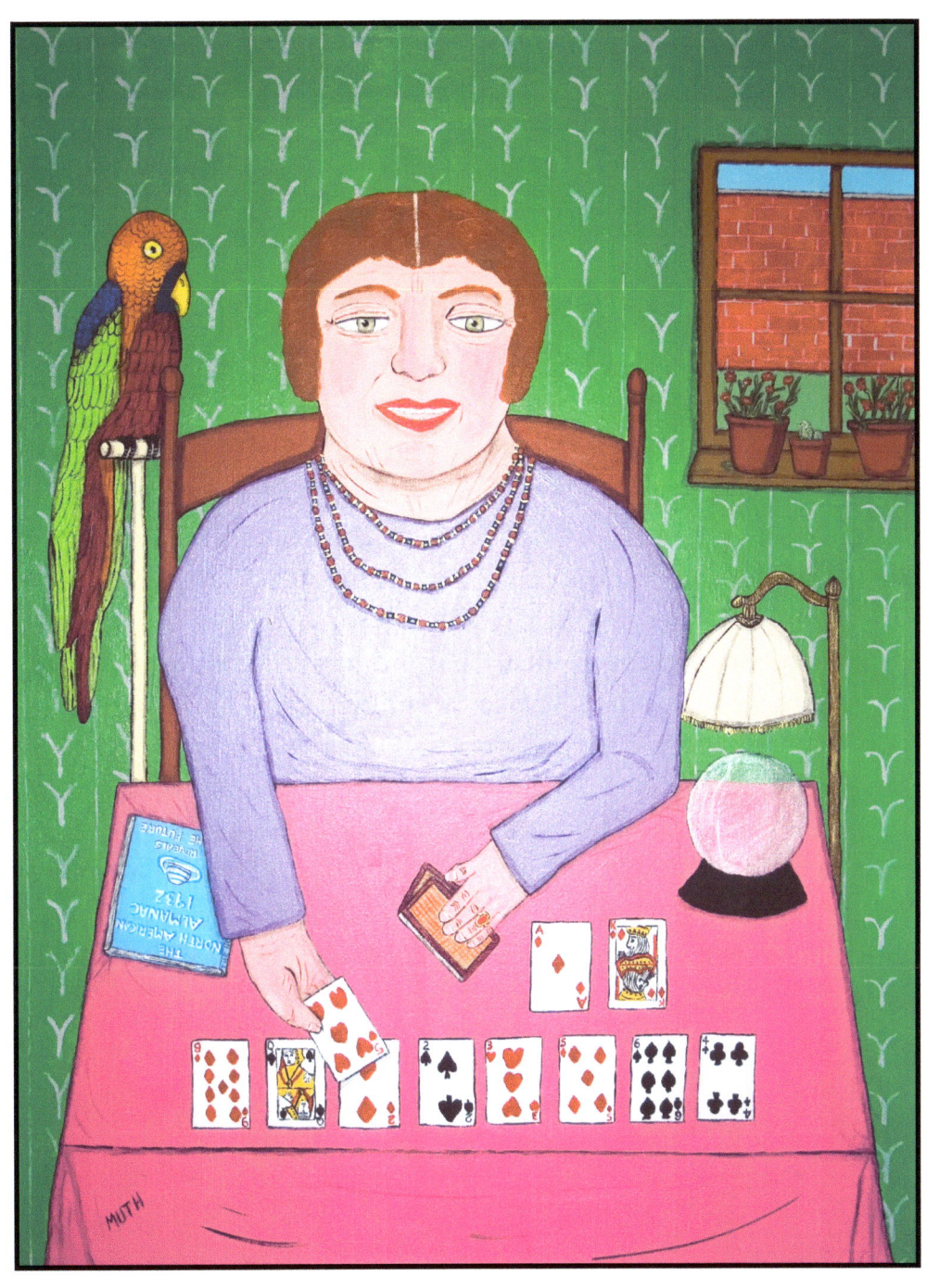

The Fortuneteller, 1987, acrylic on canvas, 24 x 18 inches *(Private Collection)*

For many years, the most popular attraction at carnivals, fairs, circus midways and amusement parks was the merry-go-round. Children and adults lined up to ride on this magical ride. It was a feast for the senses with its bright colors, lavish decorations and thrilling music. The intricately carved figures were mainly horses but often other animals were portrayed. The animals on merry-go-rounds were carved by master craftsmen known for their skill. By the second part of the twentieth century, merry-go-rounds were no longer a star feature and were broken apart or abandoned. However, a number were recovered, repaired and put into operation again as people realized they are a part of our cultural and artistic heritage. The concept of the merry-go-round goes back centuries. Another name for it is carousel which refers to an equestrian display that was popular in the seventeenth century in Italy and later in France. Riders would take their horses through elaborate circular patterns. In 1729 a merry-go-round was described as a revolving machine carrying wooden horses on which people ride. In England the merry-go-round is known as a roundabout. Well, no matter what it is called, it is an object of wonder and delight.

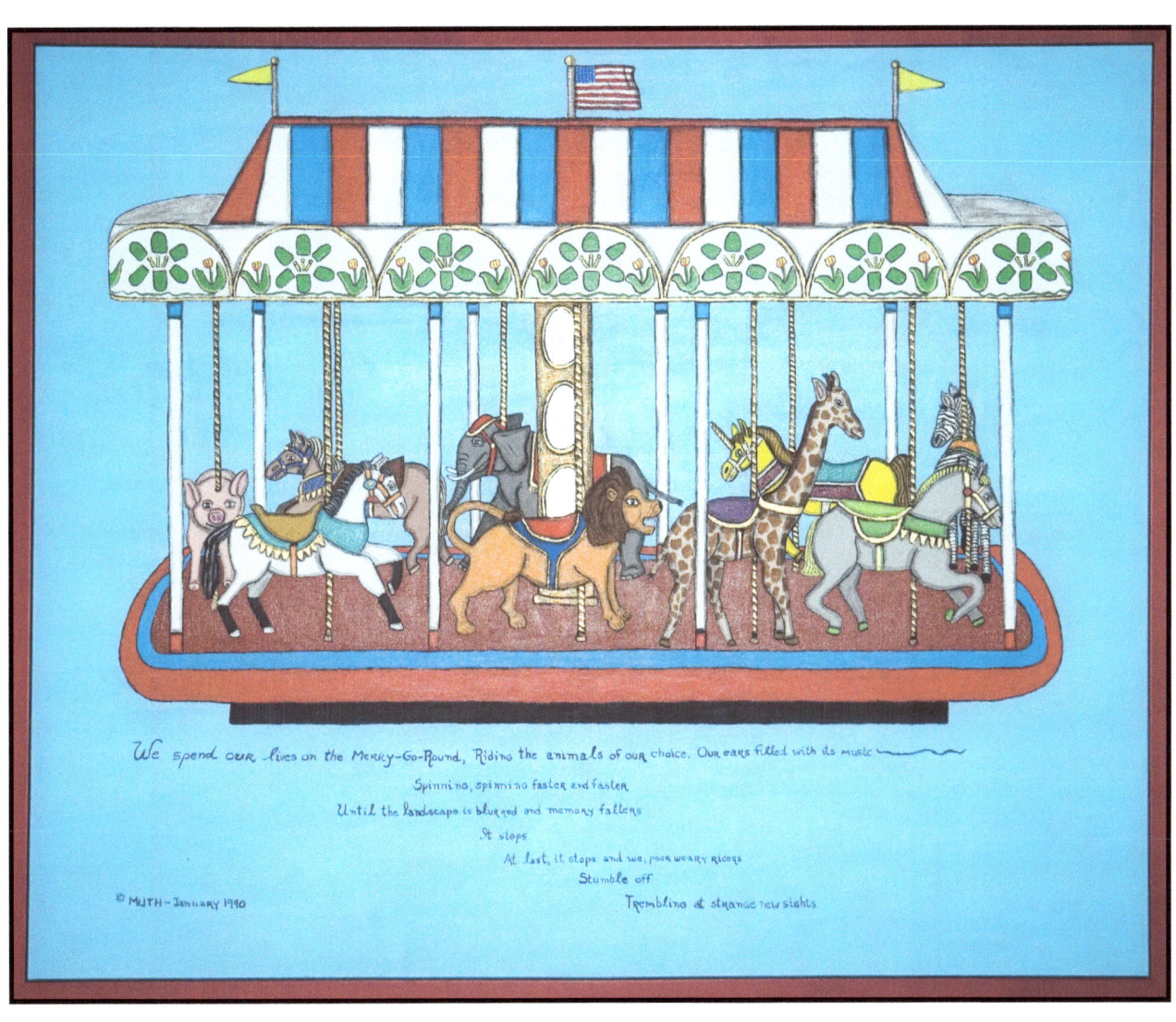

Merry-Go-Round, 1990, acrylic on canvas, 24 x 30 inches (Private Collection)

One of the great attractions when I was growing up was the zoo. At that time most of the animals were behind bars and separated by deep moats. In this picture I have an openness so that the animals could be more easily seen. The visitors are dressed in thirties styles. They represent all ages and classes. Zoos in those days were free.

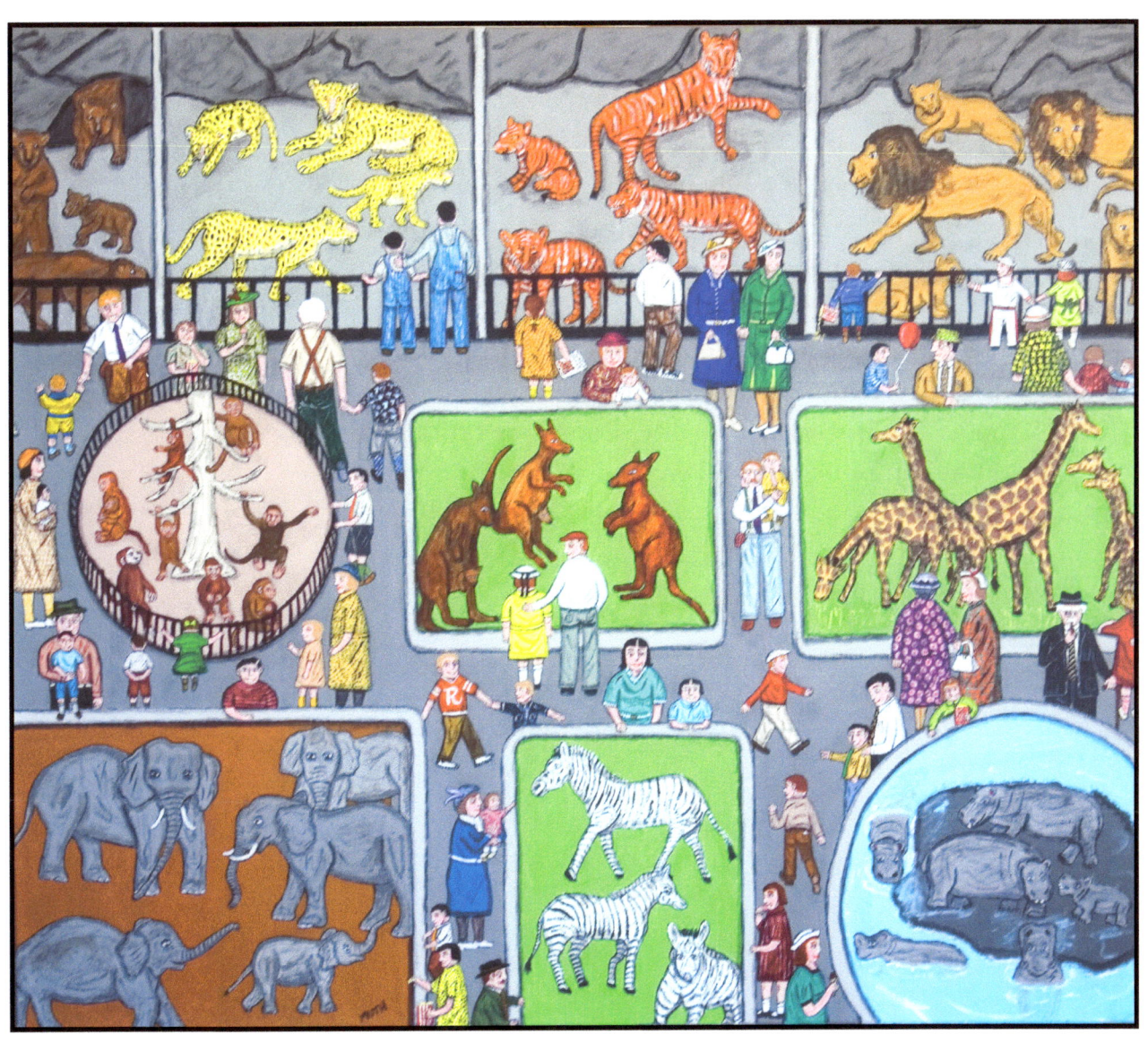

Myr-Lou Park Zoo, 199 5, acrylic on canvas, 24 x 28 inches
(Collection of Dr. Gail Kaplan and Sondra Everhart)

This shows a typical commercial street scene in the thirties. The main store, of course is the motorcycle shop. On the one side is a hardware store and on the other side is a café. A little boy is looking in the window at the display motorcycle. He has a scooter but undoubtedly he is dreaming of riding down the street on a motorcycle. There is a boy with his yo-yo and a family going by in their sedan. Mr. Capelli, a retired state policeman, is an avid motorcyclist as well as a lover of art.

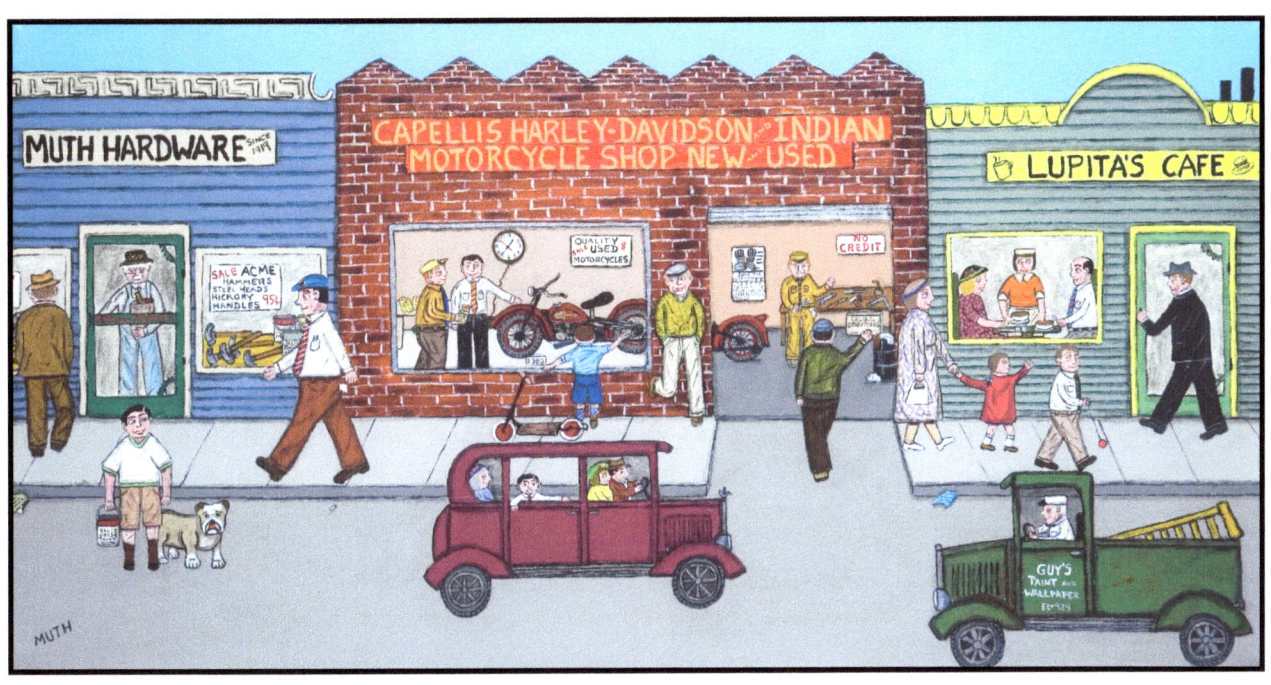

Motorcycle Shop, 2001, acrylic on canvas, 15 x 30 inches
(Collection of David and Lupita Capelli)

This painting is unique because it does not represent a personal experience. The woman who commissioned it had often been taken to the local African-American church by the lady who worked for her family. After many years it was still a vivid and loving memory for her. From her description of the place and some of the people, I was able to recreate the scene for her. The name of the church is my invention as she was no longer sure of the exact name.

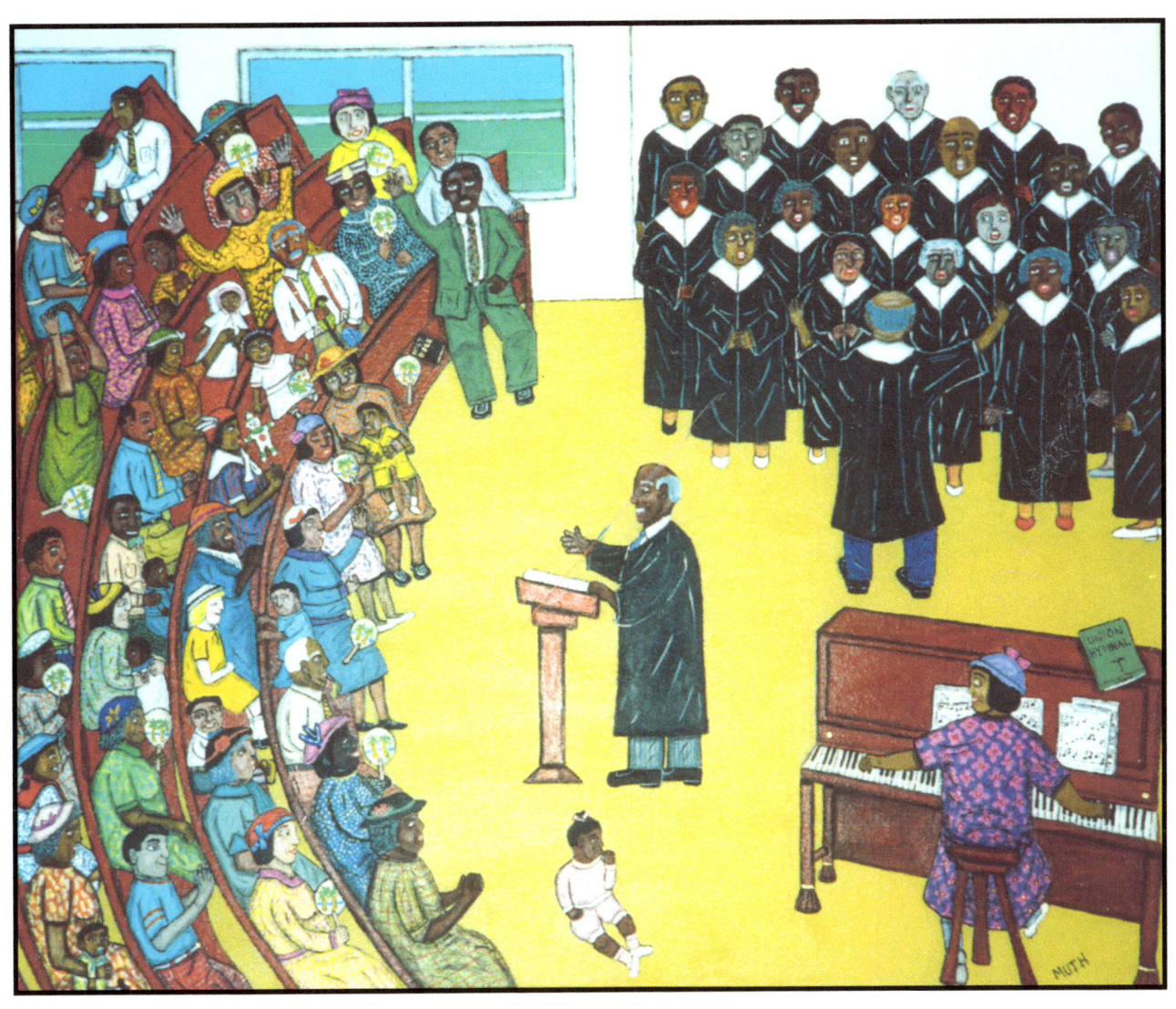

Riverview Baptist Church, 1991, acrylic on canvas, 20 x 24 inches
(Private Collection)

This book has been printed on acid free paper. The body typeface is Univers 12.5 /17. Dropcaps are Stencil Standard.